Advance Praise for
The Power of Choice

"I have had the chance to meet Melissa and hear her amazing story in person. In this book, Melissa shares insight on how she became a warrior and how she fought back to become the champion she is today. She is a great example of perseverance in the face of what appears to be insurmountable hurdles. Her love of country is strong and carries through her joining the military and representing Team USA in the Paralympic Games. A true champion in many ways."

—JACKIE JOYNER-KERSEE, Seven-time Olympic medalist

"Melissa's story of strength and courage is not only incredibly moving, it is a must-read for anyone facing any challenge. Clearly her passion for country and sport drives every one of her accomplishments. From a young gymnast like I was, to representing the United States in Paratriathlon, Melissa inspires us all with her story of overcoming unimaginable adversity and what it truly means to be unstoppable."

—SHANNON MILLER, Seven-time Olympic medalist

"Melissa's life is an unmissable story of hardship and perseverance with a message that is sure to inspire all who read it. She is someone I look up to every day—literally. I keep a photo of her on my office wall because I'm so inspired by her work ethic, personality, and never-give-up attitude. I'm proud to call her a friend and even prouder to know that our country is represented well by people like her."

—TAMMY DUCKWORTH, U.S. Senator and wounded veteran

THE POWER
OF CHOICE

THE POWER OF CHOICE

MY JOURNEY FROM
WOUNDED WARRIOR TO WORLD CHAMPION

MELISSA STOCKWELL

Post Hill
PRESS

A POST HILL PRESS BOOK

The Power of Choice:
My Journey from Wounded Warrior to World Champion
© 2020 by Melissa Stockwell
All Rights Reserved

ISBN: 978-1-64293-521-9
ISBN (eBook): 978-1-64293-522-6

Interior design and composition by Greg Johnson, Textbook Perfect

This is a work of nonfiction. All people, locations, events, and situations are portrayed to the best of the author's memory.

Post Hill Press
New York • Nashville
posthillpress.com

Published in the United States of America

*To my parents, who gave me my own power of choice
to love our country and to serve it.*

*To all of those who have worn the uniform
and the loved ones who have stood by their side.*

*And to my family, for their unwavering support
and for giving me a life I could have only dreamed of.*

CONTENTS

Prologue

April 13, 2004

I got up and put on my desert camouflage uniform, then stepped out of my trailer. As an officer, I had my own, with a single bed, and I had just put up an American flag inside.

It had been three weeks since I arrived in Iraq. I knew, from the moment I woke up that day, what I was going to do: ride along with a convoy into the Green Zone in Central Baghdad. I was a convoy commander, but, this morning, I had no real mission. I was going to take over the route the next day, so my job was to ride and observe.

There was a briefing before all the convoys left—I knew what vehicle I was going to be riding in, and I knew the driver. None of this was new. I had led everything that was going on multiple times.

Looking back, maybe I wasn't as tuned in as I normally would have been. It was a laid-back kind of day. Just learn the route, I was thinking. It was relatively easy. It was 8 a.m. About ten vehicles were lined up for the convoy. I was in a Humvee, typical for an officer, two vehicles back from the front.

The gun truck was right in front of us; their job was to sweep the road and look for any sort of abnormal activity. I would normally sit up front next to the driver, but, this morning, I was behind him in the back. Next to me was another officer, and behind us was a machine gunner, sitting out in the hot open air. We were lined up and ready to go when I saw another soldier running up.

"Ma'am, would you like me to take your door off?" he asked. "We can put a pedestal mount on."

He was talking about a piece that hooked to the side of the open door; it made it easier to point a weapon outward. Sometimes you think you're invincible. "Sure," I said.

I could smell the fuel in the air. We were slow out of the gate. The convoy commander was in the passenger seat on an electronic device watching our route, with walkie-talkie access to the gun truck in front and the vehicles behind as we picked up speed.

The area around Baghdad is just a desolate landscape: barren, some local cars, a hut that's someone's home way off in the distance.

We were moving along about ten minutes into the ride. We were all paying close attention to our surroundings. It was all still kind of surreal, but we were trained and professional. Then we came up to a bridge and overpass.

The drivers knew to swerve when they go under a bridge— there could be someone up above wanting to drop something on our vehicle. The enemy knew the smallest vehicles in the convoys are where the officers ride. My vehicle was a big target, and, as the driver swerved, it seemed to work: nothing landed on us.

But then a deafening *boom*, the loudest sound that I've ever heard, louder than anything I could ever imagine.

* * *

There was black smoke. The unmistakable smell of metal. We were wearing our seatbelts, but it was chaos, with heavy equipment sliding around the vehicle as the world rocked.

It was an Improvised Explosive Device, I realized. We hit a roadside bomb. Time slowed. The windshield smashed. We ricocheted off a guardrail as the driver tried to right us in the opposite direction. Then we crashed into an Iraqi woman's home on the side of the road.

From here on out, things are fuzzy. I can only tell you what I remember.

Chapter 1

Sweet Thunder

On my fourth birthday, my dad presented me with a big gift and a big decision. He brought home two different bikes, each with training wheels, and told me I could choose one of them. I hopped up and down in excitement as he brought two big colorful boxes in from the garage and placed them in front of me.

One was a Barbie bike, pink and girly. The other one was a bit more dramatic, with *Sweet Thunder* written in electric-looking letters. My dad stepped back and asked me which one I wanted—it was my choice.

I hesitated. This was tough. Finally, I pointed to the Barbie bike. My thinking went like this: It was pink, and, though I didn't particularly love pink things, I really wanted the basket that came with it. I could already picture it overflowing with stuffed animals, rocks, and snacks. For starters, there was my stuffed bear Woodles, who I couldn't possibly risk riding without—he would fit perfectly in there.

But my dad knew me well. While this had been presented as my choice, he gently steered me toward Sweet Thunder. When I let him know how much I cared about the Barbie accessories, he solved the problem for me—it wouldn't be hard to add a basket to Sweet Thunder, as well as a bell that would let everyone know that I was headed their way.

I was his youngest daughter, his little girl, and he wanted me to be a tough little girl. He didn't really want me to be the girl who liked Barbies and all those girly things. He saw me as the girl riding Sweet Thunder: determined, moving forward, able to keep up with everybody else.

As soon as he put Sweet Thunder together, I was whizzing around the neighborhood, loving the speed and the feeling of the wind on my face. I cruised by dozens of houses and tall pine trees and flew like crazy down a hill to a small lake that was the location of many of my tomboy adventures. It wouldn't be long before my mother would have to go out searching for me at dusk, finding me engrossed in climbing or exploring and calling to bring me back to dinner.

Sometimes you make what seems like a small choice but, looking back later, it seems so important. Sweet Thunder was the first of dozens of bikes I would own in my life, and my dad's influence in choosing it feels like it pointed the way toward so much of what happened later: my restless spirit, my embrace of adventure, the drive that always feels to me like it comes from that power to choose whenever challenges arise.

I always wore a dress in those days, even when I was riding that beloved bike. It wasn't so much of a fashion choice, though—I just couldn't stand the feeling of anything around my waist. My favorite things were running around in the woods, hunting for worms, and building forts. When I was indoors, I was a total acrobat. I had a talent for making a mess of myself, which usually involved some kind of mishap with food that I was moving too fast to bother cleaning off my clothes—who had time?

Those earliest memories almost always involve my love of sweets. This was a sweet tooth that could take on any candy and win the contest. If there was chocolate lying around, I'd eat it before anyone had a chance to scold me. Around this time, I decided to try making brownies on my own; of course, I had no idea what I was doing, and I ended up putting the brownie batter in the oven while it was still in a plastic bowl. My mom rushed into the kitchen and saved the day before the bowl melted. I was on to the next thing by then.

Picture a little spitfire who always wore a dress—that was me as a little girl. I sometimes felt distant from my big sister, Amanda, because of our age difference. She's three and a half years older than me and, pretty soon, was on to more grownup things like staying up late, shopping for clothes, or sleeping over at her friends' houses. Despite those differences, in my heart, I adored Amanda and often wanted to be her. I told my parents about this so often that they started to worry about it.

My parents always encouraged me to be my own person. They told me that it was great to be me: Melissa, a driven and determined girl who would grow up to be a strong and independent woman someday. When I got older, I would make important decisions all on my own and be the person I wanted to be without worrying about what anyone else thought.

That didn't mean I made things easy on myself. One day, Amanda and I were outside hitting a tennis ball against a backboard. She was far better at tennis than I was, and so she was able to keep me from even getting a racquet on the ball. I guess I needed to hit something, so I smashed the racquet over her head. This didn't go over well with her or my parents. It was the kind of bullheaded moment that was the flip side to my adventurousness and brashness, the side that wasn't always easy to be around.

I'd often throw embarrassing tantrums for no reason. My family took a vacation to Spain, and my parents hired a babysitter so they wouldn't have to contend with me on their own. I had outbursts on that trip, and that babysitter certainly earned her paycheck. Back home, it was time to enroll in preschool, and, while I wanted to be there every day, my mom was afraid that I'd lose my temper at some point and cause a problem. She left me for one day, then two, then three in a row without any explosions. I went along and behaved myself because I was learning something important about myself: While I thrived on high energy and restless motion, when I channeled that spirit into a busy daily routine I thrived inside. I don't even know if I would have used the word *discipline* at that point, but I loved it and craved it.

* * *

Amanda had her athletic interests that I followed with great interest. She had been on a neighborhood swim team from a young age but eventually gravitated toward tennis—even after I whacked her on the head in an unfortunate moment.

I wanted a sport of my own, something to channel my inner fire. While I was still in preschool, my mom signed me up for a tumbling class at a place called Gym Elite Gymnastics Club. But, within a couple of months, my teacher notified my mom that I was too advanced for that class and moved me to a higher level.

My earliest sports memory is probably jumping on a trampoline, gaining air and defying gravity for a just a couple of moments, then having to wait my turn impatiently until I got to go again. I hated waiting. It was so impossibly difficult to be sidelined, even for a minute, such a challenge to fight against my own impatience.

The next tumbling pass came, then another. I loved the feeling of moving through space with risky precision, the rush as my body responded to more and more difficult moves. I got serious about gymnastics pretty fast—it was really speaking to me. I rose quickly through the beginning levels and soon was told I had real potential. I was intrigued by what this meant—it sounded like another adventure, another thing to conquer.

If my parents were concerned about how much time I wanted to spend in the gym, they never showed it. Ultimately, if I was devoted to something, that was all that mattered to them. That's the kind of strength that can carry on throughout someone's life.

I also loved swimming. My mom told me that I looked like a little fish, so comfortable propelling myself underwater. I spent a lot of time at the local pool, focusing my energy on learning the strokes and feeling my muscles respond to exercise.

Stubbornness can be a good thing. Our neighborhood swim team had an age requirement of five, but, before I reached that birthday, our coach told me to try to complete a lap in an exhibition meet. I dug deep inside and made my way with total determination, my tiny arms and legs working to move me forward like a torpedo through the ocean. Every now and then, I had to stop and grab the rope by the side of the pool and catch my breath while I received encouragement from the pool deck. *I was going to do this.* I heard grownups' and kids' voices echoing in the pool, smelled the chlorine in my nose, felt the splash of water in my face, and realized no one else was going to make this happen. I might have been a little girl, but I was strong enough to reach the end.

I did it. I completed the entire length of the pool; looking back, where I'd started seemed impossibly far away. I looked up and saw that I was on the receiving end of a standing ovation from all the parents—my very first taste of the rush of winning, even though it hadn't really been a competition. I had competed against myself, finding will within. I didn't fully comprehend what I had done at the time, but I thrived off the speed and the motion—and I loved that reaction from the crowd.

The following year, I was old enough to become a member of the team. My coach had a deep Southern accent, and he used to call me Melissa Jean when he bellowed at me during practice, screaming out encouragement as I determinedly made my way through a twenty-five-yard freestyle. For a while, I lived at that pool, competing in swim meets, playing sharks and minnows with the other girls, and endlessly eating Popsicles from the snack bar. I loved that feeling of camaraderie, feeling part of something bigger than myself, and adhering to a disciplined schedule.

Then, when I turned eight, I stopped swimming. It wasn't that I didn't like it, but my advanced tumbling skills were drawing me out of the pool and into the gym. It seemed like it wouldn't be possible to excel at both. I wanted to spend all of my waking moments at the gym, even if that meant fewer Popsicles. I knew exactly what I wanted. I switched to gymnastics totally. I didn't know what it was like for other kids my age, but I already could make rapid decisions from my gut that were sturdy and sensible. It was a good thing to know what I wanted, to feel confident in making choices. It made for a strong and sturdy conscience.

Chapter 2

Finding My Limits and Breaking Through Them

Gymnastics is a difficult and demanding sport, and it doesn't let up. I didn't either. I would often come home from practice with a taped ankle or a blister on my hand from a ripped-open callus. My parents would attend to whatever the day's ailment or injury entailed. They continuously told me how tough I was, encouraging me to hang with it and keep going. They let me and Amanda do what we loved the most, and they instilled early in us that our voices were heard, our opinions mattered, and that we had the power to make our own decisions and to see through the consequences.

This felt like a transformative choice for me, establishing my individuality and ability to tackle challenges. My sister had tennis and I had gymnastics. I was drawn to the thrill of it, the feel of the beam underneath my feet. Just as I had always loved the feel of grass beneath my feet, now I loved the feel of the floor and the bars in my hands. I felt tough when I was there.

Gym Elite replaced the pool as the place where I tackled challenges and became my second home. I loved everything about it: the dry smell of the chalk, the creaking of the bars and the sounds of feet slapping the mats and the beat of the floor music providing rhythm. This is where I made new friends, and I started to practice both before and after middle school, as I grew through the grades and moved through the levels. After a while, I came and went through an exclusive back door entrance for higher-level gymnasts and worked in the sectioned-off back half of the facility. It made me feel important like I was going somewhere. In the sounds of called-out instruction and the burning in my muscles as I balanced and tumbled, I felt a sense of purpose.

By then, I was walking through the halls of Holcomb Bridge Middle School. I was Melissa the gymnast, and I'd prove it by performing my latest routine at every school talent show. It felt like I would never get enough. I channeled all my determination into the sport. It was my life.

When I turned twelve, something amazing happened. Olga Korbut, the six-time Olympic medalist, moved with her husband and son from Russia to Georgia and became a coach at Gym Elite. All of us knew Olga as the pixie with pigtails who revolutionized gymnastics with her achievements at the Munich Olympics in 1972. She was the first gymnast to perform a backflip on beam in international competition. Her groundbreaking floor routines were full of raw emotions and a connection to the crowd that helped make gymnastics one of the prime events at the Olympics. For me and other girls around the world, she had been one of the inspirations for taking up the sport and making it our own.

We waited for Olga's arrival and wondered what she would be like in person, intimidated by her legendary status. Of course, she was no longer the young girl at Munich, and we took her arrival in stride and tried to help make her feel at home in her new city. She had a thick Russian accent, and her hair was in straight bangs that were longer than in her Olympic heyday. She still very much had the body of a gymnast: strong and petite.

My family even loaned her our kitchen table when she needed help furnishing her apartment. We never got that table back—I think my parents just hoped the nice gesture would earn me some goodwill.

A few of us stood out to Olga, as she evaluated us one by one and watched us practice. We were labeled Olympic hopefuls. The other girls were both close friends and fierce competitors. I was close to Chau, who stood out for being the most flexible and having the longest legs. Dudley was noted for being really good at basically everything. They called me "Suicide," because I was known for trying the most difficult skills—and for being blind to the idea of failure.

Mind you, this didn't always mean I had the best form, or that I was going to stick every landing, but I was always up for as many twists or flips as needed—pushing through doubt and trying to find my limits and break through them.

Olga was a tough-love coach who didn't smile much. She didn't show a lot of affection, even to her own family, but I sensed she was the product of a different upbringing and that she wanted the best for us. She wanted to make us the best, and she had a warm side for those who got to know her. I felt that she adored those of us who took risks. If one of us had a callus rip off while we were on the bars, that wasn't a reason to stop. No one would ever accuse her of babying us. She wanted us to be resilient, saying: "If you don't succeed, keep trying until you do."

Many of my teammates cried in front of her, some often. I didn't dare.

* * *

One day at practice, I was trying a new element that involved a twist on the balance beam in front of Olga. Each time I did, I fell off and landed with a thud. My body hurt a little more each time, and my chest burned with frustration. I'd get back on, do it again, and fall. And again. And again.

I had fallen more than ten times when I was on the mat and trying to gather the will to get myself up on my feet. My eyes burned, and tears wanted to come out. Olga came rushing over to scream at me.

"You need to get up You need to get up right now!" she yelled. "You have the potential to be the best. Get up and do it again!"

Then she stormed off across the gym without waiting for my reaction.

I pushed against the blue floor mat and willed myself up. Her words filled me with a newfound determination. She was telling me I could be the best, not to give up. She was telling me that I had to persist. I got back onto the four-inch-wide beam and did the routine again. I failed, so I did it again. And again. Until, finally, I executed it.

The next time, I was trying a new routine on the trampoline before I moved it to the floor mat. On my first attempt, I improperly twisted and ended up nowhere near the place where I was supposed to land. It hurt, and it scared me. Olga came over and insisted I press on. By then, I would have fallen a hundred times until I got it right because I wanted to prove my worth—to both Olga and myself. The will and the choice to persevere and conquer failure became something knitted into my spirit, a channel for my restlessness.

* * *

We had a meet every few weeks and, every time, we would line up as a team as we entered the gym. We marched out onto the floor single file, shortest to tallest. In my pink leotard with a Gym Elite patch at the center of my chest, I was invariably the shortest. That made me the line leader every time, which I didn't mind at all. I paraded out proudly into the gym, under the lights, and would look to the spectator seats to find my parents' faces. I felt the need for their approval in order to compete, as though it fed me the bravery I needed.

An announcer called out our names one by one, and we stepped up and put out one arm in a salute and returned to the line before the first rotation began: vault, bars, beam, or floor.

Eventually, I got a medal in competition, and it was a moment that shaped me forever.

I stood straight. I lifted my chin. The national anthem blared from speakers overhead and I placed my hand over my heart. I looked up and there it was: the American flag. I felt an electric energy, and goosebumps overtook my body.

I was rigid with chills, thrilled and almost overwhelmed. I felt like I was floating on the podium, as though I might rise up in the air over the crowd. It was difficult to fully comprehend then, but that's the moment when my love for the American flag took hold in the center of my heart. That's when I realized how much I loved my country.

* * *

Our team started traveling the country from meet to meet. I was in competitions with gymnasts including Shannon Miller and Kerri Strug, all young women trying to be among the best in the world. I never came close to the scores earned by these gymnasts and discovered I had little chance of stacking up against their seemingly perfect performances.

Still, I kept trying. My injuries piled up, from my knees and ankles to a hairline fracture in my spine that my doctor said might worsen throughout my life if I continued my devotion to gymnastics. I was still "Suicide" at heart, though, always willing to fight through the pain and risk injury to make the next twist work, the next tumble through space with the world rushing past my eyes and ears.

We slept in hotel beds and dreamed of perfect 10s and ate at Cracker Barrels wherever we went, creating life-long good memories of hot food and friendship. Our training became even more intense when we learned that the 1996 Olympics would be coming to Atlanta—now my fantasies of a perfect 10 on the bars could take place right in my own backyard.

A local newspaper wrote about me as an Olympic "hopeful," and that was a big deal to me. I was competing at the top level by now, the highest that I could reach, but there are different ranks within elite competitors. And I wasn't the best of the best—those were the athletes who ended up representing the United States at the 1996 Atlanta Olympic games as the Magnificent Seven, the first women's gymnastics team from America to take Olympic gold.

They were my heroes, and I idolized them even though I had known them first as competitors. I watched their floor exercises over and over, memorizing them until they were probably etched in my mind forever.

* * *

But, two years before those Olympics arrived when I was fourteen, everything seemed to come to a halt. My dad sat Amanda and me on the couch in front of the fireplace we only used on rare occasions and told us that we were moving to Minnesota. This would be the fourth time we had relocated after my dad was offered a promotion; I was born in Michigan and had also lived in England when I was still very young. Dad was a corporate Chief Financial Officer, and he was always looking to advance his career and move up to better positions at bigger companies. When he saw an opportunity for himself and his family, he jumped at the chance.

Amanda was unfazed. After all, she was heading off to college soon. But I was entering high school, and I was livid.

From my dad's perspective, he was a good provider for our family and he wanted to fulfill that role as well as he possibly could. Moving around was a necessary requirement. It was hard for me to see it that way.

How could he do this to me? I stormed up the stairs and slammed my bedroom door. It felt like the end of the world.

I sat on my American flag bedspread, my eyes overflowing with tears. My mind went to my gymnastics. I was going to the state meet, and I had unrealistic visions of triumphing there and having it lead right to the Olympics. Now I knew that, by leaving Atlanta, it almost surely meant that I was losing my chance. Until then, I had prided myself on never crying when

I messed up a gymnastics routine, but now the tears came out of control when I thought about leaving Gym Elite. It burned my heart to think of not being able to honor my commitment to my coaches and teammates. Loyalty was threaded through my drives and passions, and the idea of letting them down was unbearable. Mom did her best to comfort me with promises of a good life in Minnesota. Her hugs have always had a way of making things better.

Gym Elite threw a goodbye party for us, and then we packed up our house and said goodbye to the South. I was full of teenage emotions, feeling like this was a tragedy—though, in a sense, starting high school in a new environment might have been the best thing for me.

* * *

I hadn't wanted to fully admit or understand it, but my body was wrecked and crying out for a break. I may have pushed myself to my limits in gymnastics, which wasn't a concept that came naturally to me.

We had a fancy new house in Minnesota, and I made new friends and established a welcome, regular new routine. I had friends who often hung out at my house, where I'd coax my dad into hiding his sports car in the garage when they came over; I was embarrassed that my family was living a more elegant life-style at that point than some of my peers. It didn't seem fair that some people had more than others; I was contrite about it and wanted us all to be equal.

At Eden Prairie High School, my competitive drive led me to try other sports such as diving and track while also competing on the gymnastics team—it was much less demanding on my body than Gym Elite, only a couple of hours a day, a few months out of the year. I lettered in all three sports, made all-American, and was captain of the gymnastics and diving teams.

I even tried pole vaulting my senior year—by coincidence, it was the first season high school girls were allowed to vault in Minnesota. Five of us signed up in all, and we were pretty excited to be pioneers—and I was thrilled at the prospect of the altitude and the rush of the sport. The girls had to wear helmets while the guys didn't, but we got over that inequality. I went on to compete in the state meet, with my own helmet decorated with silver, red, and blue stars that Amanda made for me. I finished third or fourth, and felt disgruntled about it, thinking I could have done better.

Still, I loved sports in high school. Maybe I wasn't "Suicide" anymore, but that spirit to break through barriers—inside and out—remained strong. I really loved my life then. Me and my friends, including Stephanie, Brandi, Katie, and Megan, who are still some of my closest friends today, spent our Friday nights at football games and our summers at the Minnesota lakes. But by the end of high school, I was ready for the next challenge.

I knew that the next step was somehow tied into my awe of the American flag. My thoughts drifted more and more to the Army, to the honor and the challenge of the military and how it was the ultimate way to represent our country. Whenever I saw someone in person or on TV wearing a military uniform, that flag captured my attention and drew me in. I thought about what it would be like to have that flag patch sewn onto my shoulder.

I went to a lot of high school and college fairs as graduation grew near. There was a West Point booth at one of them, and I took home an application.

I filled it out, then invited an Army recruiter to come to my house to talk with my parents and explain what it would take to enroll. By then, my parents were used to how patriotic I had become, and how much I had been thinking about service to my country, but I don't think they genuinely understood that I wanted to join the Army—if anything, they probably thought I was going through a phase.

The recruiter from West Point came to our house in his perfectly pressed uniform, with his military posture and a stack of pamphlets. We sat around the kitchen table as he told us about life at West Point and the doors it could open in my life. His job was to sell the military academy, and he was great at it— he talked about the tradition, the friendships and camaraderie, the physical demands, the discipline, and the challenges.

Then he looked at me straight in the eyes, calmly from across the table.

"Could you ever kill someone?" he asked.

Chapter 3

Choosing ROTC

I completed the application to West Point, but, as fate would have it, I never submitted it. My parents clearly still thought that I was just going through a phase, and they convinced me that West Point was a far-fetched goal at best. My family didn't have much of a military history; my grandfather had briefly served, but I didn't know much about it. I didn't have any military connections to make a recommendation to add to the application, and I didn't have the kind of high-level GPA or standardized test scores that would have helped make my case.

This is a moment in my life that bewilders my older self. A through-line that goes through everything since I was a little girl is pursuing anything and everything my heart points me toward as a single-minded mission, even when I know there's a decent chance that I might fail. I fancied West Point, and I saw myself there, but it was one dream that I allowed myself to let go of.

All my experiences in sports had given me a lot of hard-earned confidence—hurling myself through life and landing on my feet was something I really enjoyed. In part, I think it was my allegiance to my parents at that point that trumped my will to take chances. I always longed for their approval, and deeply valued their opinions on everything. If they were skeptical about me attending West Point, that was a barrier that kept my reckless and willful side at bay.

Instead, I enrolled at the University of Colorado at Boulder, which had been one of about ten college brochures that didn't get swept off the desk in my bedroom and into the trash by the middle of my senior year of high school. It was a big state school without a gymnastics team. My dad had persuaded me to visit there, which brought my mind back to when he gently steered me to Sweet Thunder. He's my dad, so, of course, I ached to please him and take his guidance.

And, to be fair, who wouldn't be mesmerized by Boulder? Those gorgeous mountains, those spectacular sunsets, those incredible flatiron rock formations. By the time I left that initial visit, I had felt there was truly a place in my heart that would always live in Colorado.

I was a pretty typical college freshman. I stayed out too late, sometimes drank too much, and spent a truly excessive amount of time inhaling whatever flavor was being dispensed from the dining hall's all-you-can-eat frozen yogurt machine. My roommate, Tiffany (still one of my best friends today), connected me to the crew team, which turned out to be a circle of adventuresome types who loved the outdoors and the feeling of pushing physical limits. I was really learning by this point that *downtime* was a foreign concept. I didn't judge people who spaced out on the couch or enjoyed doing nothing, but I was never going to be one of them. I had to keep moving.

I got up at four in the morning to join the crew team, dressed in several layers of clothes and gloves. We rowed in the cold waters of the reservoir, and the exercise and the feeling of motion and teamwork satisfied my soul.

That first year, something other than the mountains and the cool water by sunrise caught my eye: the ROTC cadets marching around campus. Those Reserve Officers' Training Corps students sang cadence in their spotless uniforms and looked terrifically tough and disciplined. Every time they passed by, I would stop what I was doing and watch. I had never really let go of my desire to join the Army, and I started to imagine myself as one of them. I knew that I would fit in.

Of course, at that point, my imagination didn't extend to going to war as one of them. That was the last thing on my mind.

* * *

During the winter of my freshman year, Tiffany and I were introduced to another pair of roommates. We started dating Justin and Dick shortly thereafter.

Dick was an ROTC cadet and, while I initially took him as just a soft, studious type, I soon discovered his depth and other aspects of his personality. There was something about him that was almost mysterious, an image that he seemed to want to project. He had a hard shell on the outside that seemed diffi-cult to know, but then I found out how much he loved classical music and symphonies. He had a long military history in his family.

We shared a deep sense of patriotism and devotion to our country. We loved spending the weekends off-roading in his pickup truck in the mountains outside of town, under that spectacular snow-kissed landscape and incredibly pure cool air. I knew that some people thought we were an unlikely match; I was so outgoing, and he would sit at a table all night without saying much. It was a case of opposites attracting, but it worked for us, and I fell fast. By the end of the year, we were pretty much inseparable.

We would end up breaking up halfway through sophomore year and seeing each other again later and becoming a big part of one another's lives. It was so hard to imagine the future when we were so young.

Before we broke up, though, one of the most influential things in my life took place. I was getting serious thinking about ROTC, which Dick had already joined. One day, Dick suggested that he bring me to the ROTC recruiter, and I agreed to the plan without a moment's hesitation.

We walked together through Gate 3 of Folsom Field, which was quiet and still in comparison to the Saturdays when it was home to Buffaloes football games. We went up a flight of stairs to the ROTC headquarters on the second floor, and I was impressed. The program's domain extended in a long hallway halfway around the entire stadium, lined with the offices of military personnel and cadet classrooms. It was like a secret society you would never know existed unless you were chosen and asked to join.

I had never really sat down for a serious conversation with a military officer before, so it was intimidating to introduce myself to Major Lawrence, with his serious bearing and all-business attitude. I nervously accompanied him to his office.

"You'd be joining ROTC your sophomore year," he let me know right away. "So already you'll be a year behind."

The Major sat down behind a massive desk surrounded by dozens of awards and accolades he had earned from his service. He explained that I'd have to attend basic camp, which was a three-week summer camp that simulated life in the Army. This would catch me up with all the other cadets who had an entire year of training under their belts. It sounded like a real challenge.

"Count me in," I told him.

As I left the stadium, my thoughts were preoccupied with how I was going to share the news with my parents. I had done this without their approval—and sensed they would disapprove. But I desperately wanted this. My head was spinning. My parents thought the entire concept of the Army was just a phase for me, something I would outgrow, and which would never become a reality.

Yet I also felt such clarity. This was something I had always wanted to pursue, and nothing was going to stop me. I was going to be even more restless than usual until I dealt with it, so I decided to rip off the band-aid and phoned them to deliver the news.

There was an awkward pause on the other end of the line.

"They allow girls in the Army?" my dad finally blurted out.

Of course they did, and we all knew it. I also knew this was his way to deflect from the fact that he wasn't prepared and didn't know how to properly respond. Both my parents knew how much I loved them, and how much I wanted their blessing. Honestly, I would feel wrong doing anything without them on my side.

After we got off the phone, they diligently did their research, and eventually came around to my point of view on the discipline, purpose, and learning ROTC and the Army offered. They even managed a drop or two of enthusiasm. That lessened my stress by a huge amount, and I really felt that I'd made the right choice.

Chapter 4

The Twin Towers Fall

I arrived a few months later at the Fort Knox military base in Kentucky, the one famous for the vault of gold. I would be going through basic camp at this huge, hundred-thousand-acre base, and I knew that this was going to be when I figured out whether life in the military was truly for me or not.

My barracks was home to me and dozens of other women and the place gave off an unpleasant smell of shoe polish, mothballs, and sweaty clothes. The base was full of what seemed like countless identical buildings with no decorations or frills, and the drill sergeants were terrifying—especially when they blew their whistle and gave the command to "drop and give me ten." I quickly lost count of how many push-ups I had done.

We painted our faces and toted M-16 semi-automatic rifles—this was the first time I had ever carried a gun in my life. Everywhere you looked, there were orderly formations of soldiers marching briskly around. We were yelled at, more or less, constantly—that's how it was communicated to us to do as we were told, without hesitation, no questions asked.

It dawned on me quickly that this life was even more austere than I had ever imagined. This was what it was going to be like to be a soldier.

I was like all the other cadets, dressed in identical bright yellow shirts. We shined our boots daily and made our beds with the sheet corners at perfect angles and tucked in so tightly that we could drop a quarter on the bed and watch it bounce—we really did that. We were divided into platoons where the drill sergeants were our absolute authority, hollering commands and shaping our reactions and the sharpness of our minds. They'd beat on the door and roar, and we'd be expected to scamper outside within ten minutes in full uniform with our beds made perfectly.

My favorite part of basic camp was jogging and singing cadences down the wide streets of the base, flanked by gigantic trees with branches arcing over our heads like outstretched arms. In the morning, the drill sergeant running alongside us and yelling and belting out the words in rhythm: "Left! Right! Left! Right!"

The sergeant would command one of us to lead and sing cadence, and I loved it when it was my turn. All the running was exhausting, but I thrived on it. The pouring rain, the commands, the exercise and the feeling of pushing myself through fatigue, doing this with my new friends in the platoon: It made my heart feel full for the first time, in a way that I had never felt before.

After one particular run, the sergeant squawked at us to lay on the ground. The rain pelted our eyes and our noses as we did sit-ups on the hard pavement. I felt that moment, the pain, and the challenge like they were transforming me and would last forever. It was only basic camp, but I already felt invincible. I had decided to do this. This was all me. And I loved it.

We had to pass a physical fitness test before we could officially become an ROTC cadet. It consisted of a timed two-mile run followed by all the sit-ups and push-ups we could do in two minutes. I was confident that I could pass the test, but I didn't want to simply get by—I wanted to excel and outshine everyone else.

The exam standards were calibrated by age. If you hit the maximum on each part of the test, you'd be awarded the top score of 300. But if you eclipsed the mandatory number of sit-ups and push-ups your score could go even higher. The first time around, another girl and I both scored more than 300— the highest in our platoon. That hunger for winning and that thrill of competition came back easily, and I was elated. From that time forward, we were put on a pedestal of sorts, and, whenever it was time for a fitness drill, all of the other women wanted us on their teams. It gave me a feeling of leadership and, even though I was fully aware that physical fitness was, by no means, the be-all-end-all of military life, I got a much-needed and heavy dose of confidence right at the beginning of my military journey.

I returned to Boulder for my sophomore year as an ROTC cadet, which consumed the bulk of my Tuesdays and Thursdays. Those days started with physical fitness runs and exercises, then classes that concentrated on military history, formations, and battle drills. It was required to show up in uniform, and I had to starch it so that all the seams were perfect and in place— as orderly as the halls, the classrooms, and every aspect of Army life. I began to think of all this order as looking very exquisite.

People looked at me differently when I was in my uniform. It made me hyper-aware that I was no longer a typical college student. I stood out from the crowd with that American flag patch on my shoulder—it was an emblem that represented a newly discovered purpose.

During one crisp fall day, I was headed home from class to my apartment building in my uniform when I heard the voices of my friends calling to me from up on the roof. They made a comment about my uniform, friendly but also mocking. I stood alone on the sidewalk as laughter came down from above. I tried to smile but felt awkward. They were still my friends, and some of them still are close to me today. But, in that moment, I wondered where I fit. I had one foot in a world none of them shared or understood. It felt like another turning point. I felt my smile grow more sincere as I looked up. I tromped up the stairs and joined them on the roof, feeling quite good and right about being different from the rest. This was my choice. This was my power.

* * *

Men were definitely in the majority in ROTC, and, as a result, the women in every class tended to develop even more special bonds. That year, I became close to a girl named Missy who had also grown up a gymnast and shared my tendency to be willing to go on an adventure on a moment's notice.

We called each other "Sister Bee," and really connected over the Ranger Challenge—a test of cadets' military knowledge, endurance, and skills at land navigation. The Challenge wasn't a requirement, but I saw it as a challenge and as a way of pushing the envelope and recognized the same desire in Missy when she took it as well.

The competition consisted of a two-mile run and push-ups and sit-ups—just like at Fort Knox—but also threw in timed assembly and disassembly of our M-16s and a twelve-mile ruck march with a weighted backpack with skills tests, such as throwing a grenade for distance. Missy and I trained together. We were both weakest at the run, so I'd pull her out of bed at five in the morning to jog along the rocky Boulder Creek path in the morning mist before we sprinted off to our respective classes.

We drove all the way to Kansas to compete in the Ranger Challenge, earning strange stares and laughter from other drivers along the way when we stopped to practice Army crawls and throwing heavyweights to simulate grenade tosses. We laughed in return and told each other we were building character—which we were, not to mention loyalty to one another.

* * *

There were fourteen cadets in my ROTC class on track to graduate in 2002—at that time, we'd be commissioned as second lieutenants in the United States Army. All of the training, discipline, and hardship were going to translate into a military life for real. Of course, exactly what that would mean wasn't something we understood at the time.

About a month into our senior year, I bashed my way through Missy's bedroom door.

"Wake up, wake up!" I shouted. "Come look at the TV!"

She scrambled out of bed and into the living room with the other roommates in the place we were sharing. Our eyes fixed on the TV.

We saw a long-range shot of the Manhattan skyline, so dense and beautiful in the cloudless September morning except for the plumes of terrible smoke pouring from the

World Trade Center buildings. We watched with tears in our eyes, thinking of all of the people who had died and the bravery of the police and firemen who were trying to help the trapped and wounded. And then the towers fell.

September 11, 2001. It was a Tuesday. An ROTC day. First New York, then Washington, then Pennsylvania. Our country was under attack. No one knew how bad things might still get. No one knew the number of the dead and dying.

I called my parents. Then daily routine kicked in. I put on my uniform and hopped onto my yellow-and-black road bike. I pedaled to class through the falling leaves. As I approached campus, it looked far less populated than normal, almost desolate and eerily silent. I bumped into someone I knew, and we started to talk, but the words fell away. We finally just looked at each other, too shocked to know what came next. Every movement of my body felt heavy, every syllable of speech so important that it had to be measured with care. I kept going to the stadium, running on automatic, not knowing what else to do but attend ROTC classes like I always, as though things were normal.

The atmosphere in my classroom was beyond tense. All of the cadets were sitting nervously on the edge of their chairs, tapping their boots on the floor, fixated on the huge pull-down screen at the front of the room that was running news coverage. Everyone wore a numbed, shocked expression, and no one spoke. I took my seat to join them in silence watching the tragedy that was still unfolding.

Eventually, our professor, Major Thomas, went to the front of the room and paused the TV. He looked over the room for what seemed like a long time, as though examining each of us one by one, taking in the moment before what came next.

"At the end of this year, you are going to be commissioned as officers of the United States Army," he said deliberately. "Today is going to change the trajectory of your military career. At some point, you will be deployed, and you will go to war."

The mood in the room turned even more somber and grave. Our class had recently read *Black Hawk Down*, and, of course, when we all signed up for ROTC, we knew that war was a possibility. But no one expected something as extreme, and as sudden, as the attacks of that day. The course of our lives had changed in that instant, along with the entire world. We looked around at each other with nervous smirks, eager and wanting to look brave, but also terrified. I felt a hurricane of mixed emotions: anger, fear, grief, a powerful eagerness to prove myself and to be able to rise to this moment.

Everyone in the room would be affected. The chain of events felt so powerful, so vast, so heavy with history. We would go to war.

* * *

In the weeks to come, the nation united and the spirit of patriotism that filled my own heart seemed to be everywhere. American flags went up in front of homes all over the country, and there was a sense of coming together with a shared love of what had been attacked: our stance for freedom, our values of life and liberty, our place in the world as a force for good.

The tone of our ROTC classes changed, with a stronger emphasis on what we needed to know as officers in a time of war. The professors were preparing us for a new reality. A month ago, they might have said, "If this were to happen." Now they said, "When this happens." I could sense the attitude on campus toward ROTC cadets start to change, as we were afforded more respect from our peers. I allowed myself a little swagger when I was going around campus in my military uniform.

It was a tie of unity, even on campus. America was deploying troops to Afghanistan and the Middle East, and our classmates knew very well that we cadets were going to be joining them in due time. I suppose I could have regretted joining ROTC, but, in fact, I felt just the opposite. I had longed to represent this incredible nation, and, now that it was a reality, it felt far more like an opportunity than an obligation.

Before we graduated and became Army officers, we were called upon to rank the military branches we wished to join, picking from sixteen options that ranged from infantry to transportation—the Department of Defense would then place ROTC cadets based on a combination of their preferences and the military's needs. I aspired to fly helicopters—both Black-hawks and Chinooks would suit me fine—so aviation was my top choice.

When I went for my physical, I had what felt like a major setback. I discovered that I was considered unqualified to fly by the Army because I had occasionally used an inhaler when I was a kid to deal with asthma and allergies—it turned out that was a red flag for aviation. I wasn't going to take no for an answer on this one, and my dad and I wrote to our congressman in Minnesota for help challenging the ruling. The fact was, I had allergy-induced asthma when I was a child, but I had long since grown out of it. I collected second opinions from doctors and followed all the proper channels for filing an appeal. By that winter, the appeal decision arrived in my mailbox in the form of a letter that I tore open with such force that I nearly ripped it in half.

U.S. Army Branch Assignment: Aviation.
Report for Duty: Fall 2002.

It worked. I was going to be able to serve in the place I thought I could do the most good and make an impact. For days, I would skip around whenever the very idea of flying a helicopter entered my mind: the speed, the rush, the hurling through space with control and precision.

On May 10, 2002, I received my bachelor's degree in Communications. I was commissioned into the Army the same day.

Minutes after my graduation ceremony with thousands of other students in Folsom Field, the very place where my ROTC journey had begun almost three years before, I rushed to change into my Army Class A uniform. It was a mid-length green skirt and jacket with a newly sewn patch displaying my maiden name: Hoffman.

I stood on a small stage that afternoon. Like the other graduates, I was starting a new life. Unlike so many others, it wouldn't be in the civilian world.

I raised my right arm to take the oath. *I will defend my country. I will serve with honor and respect.*

I looked down at my family and returned their smiles. When I completed the oath, I was pinned with my initial Army rank: a single gold bar that signified that I was now a Second Lieutenant in the United States Army.

It was all so sudden. I was both a college graduate *and* an Army officer.

It was astonishing to think how much my life had changed in just four years. And I would have been shocked even more deeply if I had known how much it was going to change in the four years to come.

Chapter 5

Learning to Live Without Regrets

Flight school at Fort Rucker in Alabama didn't begin until August, so I had a three-month extended stay in Boulder. Dick had been commissioned with our class and would be entering field artillery, but he was in the same boat as me, so we toiled on campus as ROTC recruiters. We ended up spending our days that summer squatting behind folding tables in high-school hallways, sweating like crazy in our uniforms as we tried to convince teenagers that ROTC would be right for them. I think I must have been a pretty good recruiter—I cherished my ROTC experience so much that I was borderline aggressive with anyone who came anywhere near our table. I'd smile and wave them over, whatever it took to connect over our shared love of our country. It wasn't terribly hard to find a way to relate anyone's interest to life in the Army, whether it was sports and exercise, discipline and routine, or personal challenges and opportunity to learn technology—I was going to woo them all.

Even though Dick and I had taken a break from our relationship, our romance was rekindled behind that recruiting table. At first, it was just dating but things turned serious again quickly—so quickly that we were engaged by August. A lot was happening all at once, and it was fairly dizzying. Agreeing to get married, winning the battle to go to aviation school—it felt like I had taken all the right roads and that everything was falling into place.

It wasn't a feeling that would last, at least not in terms of the military service I'd envisioned. My time in aviation was abruptly cut short. In contrast to other branches of the military, which require four years of active duty followed by four more years of reserve time, aviation officers owe six years of active service time—all because of the extended period it takes to learn how to fly. Dick expressed his dislike of the situation—the two of us were leaving Boulder, and I was headed to Fort Rucker to start flight school, and I would be obligated to serve two more years than him. He asked that we serve our time equally in the military so we could retire from the active Army duty at the same time and transition together into leading conventional civilian lives.

I was hesitant to see things his way at first, but the more we talked about it, the more I doubted that the six-year commitment to aviation was the right thing to do. I started to lack the gusto that had driven me to fly. On Dick's recommendation, I visited my aviation commander at Fort Rucker to request a branch transfer.

As I was making the request, I had a hard time looking into the commander's eyes, and while the words rolled off my tongue, second thoughts rattled and scattered my brain. All of a sudden, I couldn't believe what I was doing. It was like listening to someone else talk. Deep down, I didn't mean a word I was saying. I was full of contradictions.

The commander stared at me as though he was a detective interrogating a flustered suspect. He looked me up and down, a doubtful expression on his face as though something was wrong with me. No one backed out of aviation—ever. So many cadets aspired to be pilots, me included, until that day, or so I had convinced myself. I had even fought for my place by getting my congressman to intervene on my behalf. The commander had surely heard a ton of pleas from soldiers wanting to be pilots, but now here I was doing the opposite.

It was like I was under a spell. The officer had me say it again, so I did: I asked him to let me out of the program. Deep down, I knew I wasn't doing the right thing for me. I wasn't making my own decision, I wasn't listening to the choice that I knew I should be making, and I knew, from that instant, that this decision was one that I was going to regret for the rest of my life—the kind of regret that really stays with you.

Few people would ever know that I was even accepted into aviation. I never wanted to tell anybody what happened. Even then, I couldn't believe that I had backed out. I was young, I was in love. I was still learning to take charge of my own life and to make the choices my gut tells me is right. If anything good came of it, it was a firm feeling deep inside: I didn't like having regrets, and I was going to live my life with as few of them as possible.

* * *

My decision left me in limbo until a slot opened up for me in another branch of the military. It would have made things even worse to be twiddling my thumbs at Fort Rucker, so Dick and I flew to Las Vegas for a weekend getaway—there was probably no better place for distraction than the lights and crowds of Vegas.

We were having fun together, probably deepened by the serious obligations that lay ahead of us—this felt like a last fling before our service began. I woke up beside Dick on the second morning of our trip and turned over to see him wide awake and staring at me. I asked him what was going on.

"Do you want to get married today?" he asked me.

"Uh, okay," I stuttered, caught totally off guard.

"Good," he said with a big smile. "Because we have a limo coming."

To a lot of people, this might have been a silly and immature thing to do at the age of twenty-three. But it's not unusual for military people to marry so young. A lot of soldiers traditionally have impromptu weddings at courthouses or last-minute ceremonies at City Hall, so that they can be stationed at the same base. This played a big role in our thinking. I hadn't exactly expected to get married on this trip to Vegas, but now that Dick had popped the question it seemed logical enough.

It turned out that Dick had everything planned for the evening: an all-you-can-eat crab buffet for our wedding dinner, and a neon-lights limo to pick us up. I trotted around with him in my jeans and black flip-flops with a black mock turtleneck—almost as though I was secretly mourning my life as a bachelorette.

We got in the limo and I asked him where we were going. He told me to wait. I looked at him in disbelief as we turned off the highway and to a small airfield runway.

Dick pointed up ahead at a waiting helicopter that was painted in the stars and stripes of the American flag. "That's us," he said. "We're going to get married in that."

My mouth was hanging open in surprise as he took my arm and pulled me out of the limo. We jogged over to the landing pad and hopped into the waiting helicopter's open door. The rotors were raising a loud roar and dust flew everywhere in the desert heat. We squished into two tiny seats in the back and put on our headsets to get ready for takeoff. I was laughing and marveling at how unexpected and amazing all this was; I looked up front, where there was a passenger I didn't know, but things were moving too quickly to ask who he was.

We rose up over the desert, the high mountains bleached brown in the sun, the beautiful hotels and walkways of the Vegas strip below us, crowded with people, the pyramid of the Luxor and the white columns of Caesar's Palace visible below like the product of some time machine of the imagination. We circled the city, taking turns looking out the window like we were in some dream.

The passenger in front was an ordained minister and the pilot would serve as our witness. This was really happening.

Thoughts were zig-zagging and colliding with one another in my head. What the heck were we doing? Were we going to look back on this and think we were just being irresponsible? Or was this going to be the night of my dreams, the story we'd tell our kids over and over someday?

The minister recited the wedding vows over the helicopter headsets. I looked at Dick and shook my head at how wonderful and improbable all of this was.

"I do," I said.

Back on the ground, the pilot signed the paperwork. We were married, just like that. And nobody else in the world knew it. The realization that I'd gotten married without telling my parents washed over me like a wave. It was a reality that made me agitated and tense. It felt as though I was being dishonest, and that collided with my beliefs.

That feeling wasn't going to go away any time soon. The more time that passed, the more guilty I felt. My parents' approval had always been so important to me, and I kept flashing back to times in high school when my mother had agreed not to share secrets with my friends' parents to keep them out of trouble. I had opportunities to tell them as the weeks went by, but I kept losing my nerve. It wasn't that I was afraid they would be angry with me for not telling them earlier, it was the reality that I knew they would be hurt and disappointed that I hadn't confided in them from the outset.

Finally, we were all together at Thanksgiving. Before we visited for dinner, Dick and I both took off our wedding rings. The tension I was feeling was growing stronger, and it was hard to enjoy what should have been a get-together with closeness and ease before Dick and I began our service in the Army.

"Let's go around the table to say what we're thankful for," my mother suggested as Dad placed the turkey on the table and got ready to carve it.

We were all thankful for our health, for one another, for the good life we led, and the opportunities and good fortune that had come our way. When it was Dick's turn to share, he took things in another direction.

"I'm thankful for my wife," he said.

I stared at him with the same disbelief as when he told me we were getting married. I was as shocked as everyone else at the table. This was a bold move, and I had to admit that, at least, all of my worrying and guilt was now out in the open.

We fetched our wedding rings and put them on. The scene was pretty surreal for me, but then everyone at the table stood up and applauded. There were smiles and congratulations, and everyone seemed happy for us.

There was one exception. My dad had taken his seat at the table, his expression combining confusion, disappointment, and hurt. It was clear that he wasn't thrilled, and my heart ached for him. I was his youngest daughter, and every father has dreams of walking his daughter down the aisle at her wedding—not having her elope in Las Vegas and keep it a secret for months. His reaction burned into my mind, and, even as I apologized to him, it felt like a bad omen. I tried to put the thought out of my mind and enjoy the rest of Thanksgiving with my family, but there was a taste of regret.

Chapter 6

The Call of Duty

I would always regret hiding my marriage the way we did, but, in the short term, our exchange of vows paid off. After leaving Aviation, I was assigned to the branch of Transportation and completed my officer basic course in Fort Eustis, Virginia, in early 2003. Later that year, I joined Dick at Fort Hood, Texas, for my first duty assignment. As husband and wife, we could go into military life as a couple.

I was assigned to the First Cavalry Division, one of the country's most decorated combat divisions. It was started in 1921 as a horse cavalry division, and, since then, "the First Team" had served in World War II, the Korean War, the Vietnam War, and the Persian Gulf War of Operation Desert Storm. It was organized into several battalions further divided into companies, and I was going to be a platoon leader in the 27th Main Support Battalion.

The single gold bar pinned to my cap and sewed onto my uniform next to my new last name of Stockwell, marked me as a Second Lieutenant—this was regularly referred to as a "butter bar," because officers of my rank were so inexperienced that they were as likely to slip and fall on a stick of butter as to know what they were doing in a given situation.

It wasn't as though I could argue otherwise—I knew that I was raw. And, when the other soldiers would tease me, I had no choice but to take it (such as when we were having a game of paintball in our off-time and someone yelled "Get the Butter Bar" as I frantically ran down the open field).

My nerves were high that first day I reported for duty, a twenty-three-year-old classic butter bar. My job as a platoon leader meant I was going to lead twenty men and women—many of whom were older than me, and some who had served in the Army for decades. I was commissioned as an officer fresh out of college, as opposed to other soldiers who might have enlisted when they were eighteen, beginning as a private and climbing slowly up the ladder. Because of my commission, I had people under me who had experience in the Army almost as long as I had been alive. And, even though it was my first day on the job, a Sergeant Major with a quarter century in the service would have to salute me. A little backwards, don't you think?

At 0800 hours on my first day, I drove through the base's front gate and stopped to show my military ID to the security guard. He looked up and saluted me, realizing that I was an officer. I was programmed to salute back in return, of course, but I did it hesitantly. It was going to take some getting used to this officer role.

I passed soldiers in their perfectly starched uniforms with their weapons slung over their shoulders, then drove past the motor pools full of hundreds of Humvees and other military vehicles before I arrived at the 27th Main Support Battalion parking lot. Part of me was amazed that this was actually happening after so much time—I caught a glimpse of myself in a window and it took a moment for me to realize who it was.

I entered the building of my assigned company as part of the 27th MSB, Bravo Company, and was greeted by a particular Army smell—metallic, with the acrid sting of ammunition. I definitely wasn't at basic camp anymore. This place was deadly serious. If anything, Ft. Hood was more intimidating than Ft. Knox. To my surprise, though, when I met the company commander Captain Vogel, I guessed that he might have been no more than four or five years older than me. He oversaw four platoons, one of which was under my management.

Captain Vogel called me into his office and sat down, asking me what questions I had. "I'm not sure," I said. "I'm sure I'll have plenty."

He had a kind smile that went a long way toward easing my nerves. "I'll be here when you do," he told me. "I'll be here to help you with whatever you need."

There's a running joke in the Army that reflects the perception that platoon leaders don't really do much—and that it's the platoon sergeants who do all the work. I wasn't there to argue with anyone. Respect plays a major role in military life and among how soldiers view the world, and respect is something you have to earn, especially if you're a brand-new officer. I had a lot of respect for those who had more experience than I did, and I was pretty transparent about my ignorance. I already knew that, in the military, having someone's back was literally a matter of life and death; it was part of being something larger than just one person, and it meant having honesty and accountability.

As platoon leader, I was required to be very conscious about using the military chain of command, which meant that I passed information to my platoon sergeant, who led the enlisted soldiers and would relay commands and updates to the squad leaders and down to their squad members. This also meant that I wasn't authorized to directly reprimand the soldiers under my command.

My platoon sergeant was Sergeant First Class Freeman, a tall, lanky African-American man who struck me as astute with a quiet demeanor. I had a feeling, from the beginning, that he would be on my side and an important ally. My gut told me that I could trust and confide in him, and he seemed straightforward and focused on the job at hand. I vowed to myself that I would earn his respect and that we would be a good team. I also knew how much I needed his help. I had been trained, but only by the book—and SFC Freeman had fifteen years of Army service under his belt. Our knowledge gap was similar to that between a child and a kind babysitter.

A true leader admits when he or she doesn't know every-thing. Part of that is not being hesitant to ask for help, which meant digging into my reserves of humility. Cultivating healthy honesty and openness with Sergeant Freeman was going to help me a lot more than adopting an arrogant attitude. That wasn't going to be too hard—it was impossible not to respect the sergeant—but it would also mean putting my stubbornness and impatience aside.

I was glad that I knew myself well enough to resist bluffing or using my rank to get my way. I worked closely with Sergeant Freeman in those months, and I gradually started to earn his full respect. And he was able to be honest with me as well. One afternoon, I came across some of my soldiers talking and goofing around when they were supposed to be at work. I reprimanded them on the spot, which seemed like the right thing to do. Later that day, though, the sergeant pulled me aside.

"Ma'am, you can't do that," he said. "That's my job. You come to me first, and then I'll take care of it for you. It's the chain of command."

I suppose I could have pushed back and said that I was going to discipline the soldiers the way I saw fit, but I agreed with him that I needed to remember the proper channels. I told him that I had made a mistake, that I was a young Second Lieutenant, and that I appreciated he felt our communication was good enough that he came to me about it. It was a little thing, but those moments started to gather momentum and we were able to work well together.

I learned a lot about leadership in those early months, as I also tried to earn the respect of my platoon. My soldiers called me "LT," shorthand for "Lieutenant." I itched for all of them to like me, to trust me, to think that I was cool. But they couldn't think that I was going to be their friend, because I also had to require them to obey me. Walking that fine line and trying to cultivate nurturing relationships with the younger soldiers was tricky.

Some of the younger soldiers had visions of military glory. They were reckless and cocky like Tom Cruise's Maverick in *Top Gun*. Others were quiet and tentative, with doubt in their eyes, and they stood silently waiting for me to tell them what to do. Whenever I had a chance, I would talk to the other platoon leaders who were in the identical situation as mine, and we would compare notes. Sometimes it had to do with motivating a particular soldier or having to deal with those men who didn't like being told what to do by a female officer.

The days at a U.S. Army base are unbelievably monotonous. Fort Hood was no different than any other in that regard. We started every morning with our physical training (PT) formation at 0630 hours, dressed in our gray Army shirts and black shorts and standing at attention on big concrete slabs behind our building. We might spend the afternoon in our vehicle maintenance and transportation courses, then end up closing the day with another company formation at 1700 hours. Then came the familiar sound of "Retreat," the Army ritual of a blaring bugle call along with the lowering of the flag—it signified that I had made it through another day and that I had a little bit more experience under my belt.

Even if I wasn't in formation at the time—I might be driving around the base, for instance—it was customary to stop what I was doing, pull my vehicle over to the side of the road, and salute in the direction of the flag. The entire base came to a standstill as every soldier did the same—a precious few minutes of focus and contemplation of the values we all shared and the mission that had brought us together. The discipline of routine had begun instilled in the deepest parts of my being, and it was a major aspect of the cohesion and sense of unbreakable bond that characterized military life.

I had come a long way from the ragtag, willful little girl racing around my neighborhood outside Atlanta, but that restless spirit still sought a way to express herself. Looking at the flag in the lengthening shadows of the early evening, I would salute everything that it stood for, all that it had brought me, and the hopes that I would continue to be able to live up to it.

Chapter 7

Deployment

All of the soldiers under my command were trained in the Transportation Branch. This meant that Transportation was either their chosen branch or that they didn't necessarily come into the service with the highest test scores, which could be for a variety of reasons. When soldiers enlist, they take the Armed Services Vocational Aptitude Battery (ASVAB), which is a test that assesses each individual's qualifications and where they fit best in the service.

Without necessarily judging anyone, I couldn't help but notice that some of my soldiers were overweight by military standards—even though I believed that those standards could set unrealistic expectations. There were detailed graphs saying that if a person was a certain height they should fall within a certain range of weight. If someone came in over that weight, what came next was known as the tape test—you'd get a measuring tape around your major muscle groups to try to determine if your weight was over because of muscle mass (because muscle weighs more). If that was the case, you'd get an exemption. If not, you were put on a list, entered into a weight-loss program, and tested more often than those who fit the graphs.

There was no getting around the fact that you have to be physically fit in order to be an effective soldier. This didn't keep some of my soldiers from having alibis for why they couldn't participate in daily workouts: they had a sore ankle from the day before, or the doctor had said they needed to take the week off. I'm not one for excuses, and I got pretty good at pretending not to hear them. I thought they should consider themselves lucky they didn't have to survive a week of work-outs at Gym Elite.

Managing and encouraging the soldiers on a daily basis was a definite challenge, and some of them came into the service without much experience with routine, discipline, or daily exercise. I had to look at it as a daily challenge, just more items to add to the to-do list in my head to keep me occupied all the time.

There were times when I wanted to push them more, knowing how much value I got from pushing through physical and mental barriers. One sunny morning at PT, I elected to lead a platoon run. Even though I had never considered myself a particularly fast runner, I was determined. I started out with my soldiers running right behind me and set what I thought was a reasonable pace—this was without a weighted backpack. I turned around about five minutes later, and no one was there. I was all by myself. Not one of them had been able to keep up.

I kept running anyway. They'd meet me at the finish line, and I hoped that my pace would inspire them to try harder next time. If we were going to be in the trenches together, we'd need to rely on this kind of hard support, working through all our different faults and shortcomings, pushing through barriers and the walls that our minds and bodies erect for us.

It was important that they knew I had high standards, and that I would back them, no matter what. If I had to set the pace, they'd also know they had my undying loyalty.

* * *

The Iraq War started in March of 2003, a year and a half after the attacks of September 11. There were already transportation units that had been deployed over there, and we were preparing for the possibility of going to war by going through battle drills: leading soldiers in training field exercises with fake villages, where we would drive our vehicles through simulated situations to reflect what it might be like there. Still, we had no idea when we would be implementing them, so we lived with a lot of daily anticipation and uncertainty. I kept focused on routine and discipline.

It was going to happen one day. We were going to Iraq, and we knew it; it was just a matter of when. We'd drive our caravan of vehicles along a long dusty road. The lookout would spot someone hanging out the window of a building, and then we'd have to determine how to react. Were they the enemy? Were they harmless? How would we know the difference? Were they just an ordinary person going about their day, or were they about to toss a grenade into our vehicle? If they did, what were we going to do about it?

The exercises focused the mind, sharpened reactions. But they weren't the real thing, and you could only prepare so much for the totally unexpected.

In January 2004, the order came down that our First Calvary Division was going to deploy. I had imagined this day for so long and, in so many ways, wondered how it would feel and how it would affect those around me and under my command. In truth, the day was pretty much a blur. Dick was also in the same Division, so we were going to be deployed together—that overshadowed everything else, that we were going to be embarking on this new reality together.

I called my family and friends. "I'm going over," I told them one by one. I emailed basically everyone on my contact list and told them the same.

When I heard the voices on the other end of the line, it felt as though they were more shaken up than I was. Of course, they hadn't been trained to accept this reality for all the months that I had. It occurred to me that maybe I had known all along that this was going to happen—all the way back to when I had taken home that West Point application. It had been my future, and now it was reality. It felt like fate.

Everything escalated after that moment, like a gust of wind was blowing my whole life forward in a way that I'd never experienced. The days on the base became longer and more intense. The battle drills were stepped up a notch. A sense of anticipation and electricity seemed to be running through everyone on the base. Many of my soldiers had signed up for the Army because they wanted to go to war, to be the tough kid who left high school for Iraq with their gun at the ready.

Me? I was excited to be wearing that American flag patch on my shoulder. I was a ball of nerves, to tell the truth, but I was also ready to do whatever was needed to defend the country I loved so much. I felt that I was going into combat for a legitimate purpose. I didn't feel full of what you would call fear, but I felt a sense of caution. This was going to be a level of danger so far removed from anything in civilian life I had known. I needed to be smart.

We would be in Iraq for a full year, a tour that would begin in March. The first step was shipping over any supplies we would need. That meant mobilizing our trucks, painting the Army-green vehicles desert camouflage, and filling huge metal cargo containers called connexes with supplies and ammunition before they were loaded onto a train that would take them by rail to the sea where they'd be shipped to Iraq.

It was a lot of work. Each soldier was also allowed to pack two duffel bags with personal items. That wasn't much, so I had to be practical. I filled mine with the essentials: uniforms, boots, brown undershirts, long- and short-sleeved shirts, and my American flag. The word was that the insects were really bad over there, so the future mother in me spent an entire day soaking both my uniforms and Dick's in bug repellent.

There were other logistics to think through. U.S. soldiers weren't permitted to carry cell phones in Iraq at the time. We'd have access to email, but we really had no idea how much computer time we might be able to carve out. So Dick came up with a clever idea: We'd each pack small black walkie-talkies in our duffel bags—since we wouldn't be stationed too far from each other, we might get to talk to each other that way.

Dick was going to be in Central Baghdad, while I would be less than twenty miles north of there in Taji. We would leave our walkie-talkies turned on at all times, so that, when we got in range of one another, we could hear them crackle.

* * *

On March 8, we went to war. Dick's battalion was leaving two days after mine, so he walked over to my company building that morning to see me off.

"I don't know when I'm going to see you next," he told me. "But I know that it'll be in Iraq."

In that moment, all the giddy bravado and euphoria of anticipation was destroyed in an instant. We hugged outside Bravo building, such a familiar feeling but now so different. I remembered scenes like this from movies, when loved ones said their tear-filled goodbyes before going off to war. But this was different. We were both going. That meant double the tears, double the worry, double the jitters.

The moment etched itself in my mind. I felt the warmth of the sun, a slight breeze. I felt Dick's familiar arms around me and was almost overpowered with emotion.

We really didn't know when we would see each other next. We were both trying to be strong and to hold back the tears. We did an okay job. We said our goodbyes, and then I accompanied my fellow platoon leaders to breakfast.

Our final breakfast at Ft. Hood was at the fast-food joint Popeye's. It was a popular spot, and the line wrapped around the whole restaurant.

On nearly every U.S. military base, there are a handful of fast-food chain restaurants where the soldiers congregate. Because so many of us were being deployed that morning, Popeye's was taxed to capacity. It was really a last taste of the states before hitting the road for the unknown. Dozens of military personnel were in line, all in the desert camouflage uniforms that marked them for deployment. The air was alive with excitement and uncertainty, with a fair amount of bluster to hide a soldier's natural nervousness.

We scarfed down chicken and biscuits before we were loaded up on a band of yellow school buses that took us in a caravan to an airstrip where a big United Airlines plane was waiting. Some of the soldiers' families were there, and there was waving and crying as we boarded the plane in our bulletproof vests. Our weapons were unloaded and stored in the safe position. As an officer, I was seated at the front of the plane in First Class, another reminder of the military hierarchy that felt strange that afternoon.

I felt like I didn't deserve it. If anything, it should have been Sergeant Freeman sitting in First Class. But military rules were military rules, and this wasn't like the time I asked my dad to hide his sports car in the garage so that we could at least enjoy the appearance of everyone being more equal.

I sat down next to Lieutenant Woodward, the platoon leader for Alpha Company. I enjoyed his presence. He was a little bit dorky, in a likable and fun way, with his blond hair and glasses. He was also a devoted soldier, trustworthy and dependable— how much, I would eventually learn.

The plane took off into the sky of an afternoon that must have looked like any other to most of the people in the world. We sat in silence, with the hours going by as Lieutenant Woodward and I watched the map on the TV in front of us, where a little blip of an airplane traces the long route from Texas to Kuwait.

* * *

Our plane made a pitstop in Greenland to refuel and we were allowed off the plane for a brief respite. I stopped for a moment in front of the Starbucks at the airport—chock full of soldiers in uniform waiting for a caffeine fix. There were so many moments that I wanted to fix in my memory, these places and these military personnel going to parts unknown. Then we took off for the second half of our journey.

Back in the sky, to my delight, we flew high into the night and saw the Northern Lights. They were a vivid pink and purple in the dark sky, and the pilot invited a couple of us to the cockpit to take in the view. I was so moved that my eyes burned. I had never seen anything so beautiful. It was like we were literally flying through pink and purple streamers falling and pulsating from the heavens, like a scene from *Mary Poppins* or some fantasy where we were entering a different world of dreams.

It was what seemed like many hours later when we landed smack in the middle of the Kuwait desert.

Holy crap.

I was there. I was right next door to the war.

I stepped off the plane, weapon in hand, and into the boiling hot air of a land that I had studied for so long. My nervousness only added to the sweat I broke without moving in the afternoon sun—like the hottest day of the year back home, only drier and even more sweltering. I carried my equipment, which felt heavier than ever, realizing the magnitude and reality of the moment. It had been just more than a year since the U.S. military invaded the region. Now I was standing in the middle of that history, and I was going to be a part of it.

But I was also frightened. Being patriotic and driven didn't mean not understanding danger. In typical Army fashion, I had some time to think about it. We went into hurry-up-and-wait mode before the buses arrived to take us to our base in Kuwait, where we would be for a few weeks until shipping out to Iraq. At least our gear and belongings would be waiting there for us. I had been in the Army long enough to know how super-important it was to be on time at any cost—then be prepared to wait for hours for whatever came next.

I still wasn't any more patient than I had been at any other time in my life.

The other platoon leaders and I ended up with downtime in that hot, dry, sunbaked air, so we decided to cheer ourselves up by getting something to eat. We made our way to an outdoor space, where we wandered through signs in Arabic—it was like a mall made up of white tents, kind of like a farmer's market but plopped into the desert.

"I don't believe it," I said when we looked ahead.

There was a familiar sign: Subway sandwiches.

I pulled out my wallet. I had a bunch of coupons and stamps inside from the Subway at Fort Hood. We went inside, where it turned out the cashier spoke English.

I pulled the coupons out of my wallet and put them on the counter when I reached the front of the line. "Do you guys take these?" I asked.

He smiled. "Yes. We absolutely do."

So my first encounter in the nation of Kuwait was getting a discount Subway sandwich with coupons I had brought from America. So far, my deployment was off to a great start.

I hope everything over here is as easy as this was, I thought to myself as I chowed down my chicken teriyaki sandwich. It felt like I was at the beginning of a long winning streak, bound for the easiest deployment in history.

Chapter 8

Wolfpack

We spent three weeks in Kuwait before we took the long three-day convoy trip into Iraq and to my Forward Operating Base, and new home, of Taji. Before we left Kuwait, Dick and I carved out an hour at a little shopping center, where I bought a lighter with Saddam's face on it. It dropped bombs on his head when you opened it and fired it up—you take humor where you can get it in a war zone.

Driving over the lines from Kuwait to Iraq was nerve-wracking, and my heart started to beat a little faster. We drove down barren dirt roads through the bustling city of Baghdad and then finally through the gates of Taji. When I first arrived at Taji and set up my new home, I was one of about a hundred soldiers who were occupying the same temporary living space of a large hangar filled with cots—not exactly luxury accommodations.

My company was called Wolfpack; our company commander was in charge of four platoon leaders, with me being in charge of the third platoon. I hoped that we'd live up to the Wolfpack name in looking out for one another. The airfield and the base were in a pretty rough neighborhood, which was known as the Sunni Triangle. When Saddam Hussein was in power, it used to be a base for his Iraqi Republican Guard, and we were told that it used to be a place where Saddam's government manufactured illegal chemical weapons. The base had come under American control during the invasion the year before.

The whole base was still pretty desolate and bare, with a scattering of warehouses and trailers as the facility was being ramped up for heavier use. Eventually, the place would have gyms for the soldiers, as well as buildings in which they could hang out and relax and stores where they could buy food and magazines from back home. I'd later hear they even installed a pool, but, when I arrived, none of that was there. There was mostly heat, sun, and a feeling of tension in the air.

For me, it was apparent from the first day that the climate and the smells in this part of Iraq were going to be less than delightful. It was a dusty, war-torn country that had been through a lot over the previous decades. The smell of burning trash seemed to always be in the air. The heat seemed to never let up. It was a dry heat, like baking in an oven, and when you were in a full-body uniform carrying gear it was impossible to get comfortable. We were also smack in the middle of the desert. You could pretty much only see sand in all directions, broken up only by the bunkers that were in place, in case rocket-propelled grenades would come soaring in seemingly out of nowhere.

When that happened, there was a particular whistle you would hear. It meant that it was time to run—and run now—into the bunker until the noise passed and you were given the "all clear" to resume whatever you were doing. It would rattle anyone's nerves. Those rocket-propelled grenades would come in the middle of the night and interrupt our sleep. They sounded like train whistles back home, the way that high-pitched whine would get higher and louder as it got closer and closer.

My first night in Iraq, I was lying in my cot when we heard that sound for the first time. My heart immediately started to pound in my chest—the fight-or-flight reaction. We were all new, and so we scurried for shelter under our cots. Those were made of canvas and metal frames and wouldn't protect us from anything.

"Into the bunker!" yelled one of the more experienced soldiers, pointing the way.

The bunker was lined with sandbags. We tumbled in and held our breath, waiting for the danger to pass. There were some things that classes and basic courses really couldn't prepare you for.

That sound became all too familiar, all too quickly, and in case anyone doubted we were in a war zone, it put that ambiguity to rest.

* * *

There was a line of about sixteen payphones that represented our only way of calling home and hearing familiar voices since cell phones weren't allowed. Most of us kept calling cards in our pockets so we could pay for those precious calls, but there was always a line of soldiers at the payphones stretching to forever. There also wasn't a lot of downtime built into the day to wait for everyone else to have a much-needed conversation with a parent, a spouse, a child—those voices of familiarity that gave all of us courage and bolstered our will.

Whenever I was able to reach my parents, I tried to downplay how eerie and petrifying I found this country.

"What's it like over there?" my mother asked.

I thought for a second. *It's a war zone. People are here who are trying to blow us up. Everyone in this country speaks a language I don't understand. It's so hot and sandy that I have to rub the grit out of my eyes for fifteen minutes before I can even try to sleep.*

"We're hanging tough," I said.

The regularity and training of military life are designed, in part, to help an individual soldier cope with the fear of being in a situation such as war. Our daily tasks included driving transportation routes with multiple other vehicles in convoys. There were always Iraqis along the side of the road, watching us. It was impossible to tell what they were thinking, or what their intentions were. Rumors were rampant every day of insurgents who were trying to climb over the fences to attack our base.

"We've got it under control," I told my mom. "Don't worry."

* * *

Dick and I got to see each other twice during those earliest days in Iraq. One time, the walkie-talkie I carried from him unexpectedly crackled, and we were able to find each other for a quick hello under the desert sun. It did us both a lot of good to see each other; for a moment, here and there, it was like we were back home behind those ROTC tables, just enjoying each other's company and believing in what we were doing together.

Moments of comfort in a war zone, though, were few and far between. Surrounded by soldiers from all around the United

States, from all kinds of cultures and backgrounds, really did drive home why we were there and the fact that we would all look out for each other. We needed it. The concept of death felt close many times a day.

A couple of nights later, I was longing again to hear my parents' voices, even if it meant downplaying how I was really feeling. Comfort and reassurance felt like gas in a tank, and I needed to be filled up and topped off.

The line to the phones was long as usual, but I couldn't get angry about it. Everyone was there for the same reason: that lifeline of the voice of a loved one. I tried to be patient, standing there sweating in my full uniform with the day feeling like it was passing me by. I was about halfway to the front and counting every minute.

"Wolfpack three-six," came my company commander's voice over my second walkie-talkie—the one issued by my company.

I blinked in the heat and felt my jaw tighten. Wolfpack 3-6 was my individual call sign. The "3" meant the third platoon, and the "6" was reserved for platoon leaders.

"Wolfpack three-six," the voice repeated.

I looked at the bank of phones. I wasn't going to get to the front that day. I stepped out of the line and took my walkie-talkie off my belt loop.

"Wolfpack three-six here," I said. I took one last look at the other soldiers talking to someone from home, their eyes lit up, some smiling, some crying. I felt good for them. Then I got back to work, trying to hear those voices from home in my head.

* * *

In April, about three weeks into my deployment, my living conditions underwent a huge improvement. I got to move into a new, single-wide trailer, which I had all to myself. A place all my own, it had three steps up to a space with a twin bed and a desk. It felt like total luxury, and I didn't regret saying goodbye to my cot in the hangar. The trailer also had air conditioning, which was amazing. After getting so accustomed to being around other people pretty much every hour of the day, for a moment, I worried that my new home might get lonely.

I hung up my American flag over my desk, and that gave me a feeling of being home. There was plenty of fear and uncertainty in being deployed in a war, along with homesickness. But I still had the strong and powerful feeling that had risen in my heart when I stood up on that podium when I was a girl after the gymnastics competition, with the national anthem stirring up the patriotism and pride that would stay with me everywhere I went. I believed in my soul in everything that the flag stands for, and that allegiance was a true source of courage. Of course, as I moved into my trailer and thought it was going to be for the long haul, I had no real idea of how much resilience I was going to have to find inside myself.

Chapter 9

A Patriot with Protection

April 13. I woke to the sound of my alarm at 0600 hours. Another day in the desert.

This morning, for whatever reason, I felt invincible. I was getting into a rhythm in my deployment. I'd started to feel ready for whatever happened, that I could handle whatever came up. I had faith that we were all going to make it home safely.

In all, I had sixteen convoys under my belt, since I'd arrived just a few weeks earlier. We'd already covered a lot of ground. We were starting to work with more and more confidence. I liked how busy we stayed, the way the days were starting to go by with order and regularity. I liked the fact that a big part of my job in the Army was to lead my troops by keeping moving, staying active, getting things done.

My battalion supported others in the area, which meant that we'd transport supplies to different camps in the area. We'd drop them off, spend a day at that camp, then make our way back to our base. The convoys were moving nonstop. It was part of the vast supply chain of the entire United States Army in Iraq, which was a massively complicated undertaking of which we were only a part.

I kept a convoy tally on the wide-brimmed Army issue hat that I wore all day to block out that blinding sun. If it was a convoy that went off without an incident of any kind, I tallied it with a black tick mark using a pen. A convoy with an incident would be tallied with a red tick mark. So far, my hat had fifteen black marks and one red one. That single incident so far had occurred when one of my drivers had to shoot his weapon when we saw some suspicious activity on the road. Thankfully, no one that day had been injured or hurt.

We changed supply routes every three weeks, which I liked for the variety. Today, it was my job to do a ride-along and learn the ins and outs of the latest route. It was relatively easy, kind of like a shift-change day, not a lot of pressure.

The day started like most of them did by that point. I grabbed my blue Chapstick, applied it to my dry lips, and dropped it into the pocket of my desert Army fatigues. I jogged down the three steps from my trailer to the ground. I was wearing my desert camouflage uniform and my bulletproof vest.

At 0630 hours, I joined the other soldiers at the DFAC, the chow hall, where we stuffed our faces with fuel for the day ahead: scrambled eggs, bacon, pancakes, lots of black coffee. The place was packed, and the sounds of chow being served up competed with voices and occasional bursts of laughter. It might not have been much, but it was starting to feel like home. It was the Army, and everyone by then had learned to eat fast. No one lingered over their coffee in the DFAC.

We gathered for the daily briefing at 0700 hours, just like we did every day. Since we were a Forward Operating Base, the information given to me and the other officers relayed the missions for the day, as well as the previous day's casualties. I stood in the hot desert sun with the other platoon leaders, listening to the names being read off, hoping there wouldn't be any familiar ones on the list but also feeling the loss of each. If we didn't hear a name we recognized, it almost became a roll call of sorts. We had started to almost become immune to the feelings it stirred up because there was simply too much to think about.

That morning, I heard a name that snapped me to attention: Renina Miller.

"Wait," I called out. "Can you say that name again?"

They said her name again. Renina had been in my officer basic course. She had been shot in the butt. A wave of chills came over my body, and I felt a lightheadedness that told me I needed to breathe and calm myself down. I tried to think it through. Renina taking fire made it all the more real that I was in the same danger.

Renina was in charge of a platoon with really large Heavy Equipment Transport (HET) vehicles. Those things moved slowly and were considered easy targets for insurgents. My platoon ran a faster Load Handling System (LHS) and five-ton trucks in our convoys—we moved quicker and were harder to hit.

Nothing would ever happen to me. Tragic events always happened to someone else. There was no way my name was going to come up on the daily briefing list.

* * *

The Captain explained that we'd be going on a ten-vehicle convoy from Taji to Central Baghdad—right into the famous

Green Zone as a routine convoy delivering supplies. From the sound of it, it was shaping up to be a fun day.

We'd all been waiting to go to the Green Zone. It was the American bubble. It was a nearly four-mile demarcated area in the center of the city that had become the hub of U.S. military command following the invasion the year before. Before that, it had been the seat of Saddam Hussein's power, and all of his important presidential palaces and monuments were there. The big one was the Republican Palace, where Saddam had greeted or confronted other heads of state and his own ministers and generals. Everyone had seen the Green Zone all over the news in photos and videos, and everyone talked about it all the time, so we were all massively excited to be going there. We were spending every day in a country that we all considered scary, so this adventure was a welcome diversion—and a chance to see even more history.

There were always security concerns, such as large contingents of Iraqi insurgents, or unknown objects that had been spotted by surveillance along the roads. We got a routine update and then headed to our convoy vehicles to prepare for departure.

As a convoy commander, ordinarily, I'd be busy communicating with headquarters as soon as I got in my vehicle, getting and giving updates, making sure things were going as planned. But, this morning, I didn't have a specific role to play. I'd be taking over this supply route tomorrow, so, today, my job was to tag along, observe, and learn. I'd have to commit the route to memory, but I was getting good at that.

I even brought my camera along. I didn't know if I'd exactly say I was looking forward to "fun" headed for the Green Zone, but I wanted to document the things I saw.

It was right around 0800 hours when my nose let me know that our convoy was starting up. Yes, it was noisy, but the smell brought me into a state of heightened awareness. I closed my eyes for a couple of seconds and took it in. The smell of diesel gas mixed with the rising heat of the morning and the feel of metal already hot from the sun.

My vehicle was the second from the front, and it was the smallest one in the convoy. The officers were usually in this spot, making it easy for us to see what was going on and to relay information to the vehicles behind us. Of course, the Iraqis also knew this, which made us targets. This was the kind of information I didn't share with my parents when we talked on the phone.

I was in a Humvee, standard for an officer, and it was sandwiched in the convoy of LHS vehicles with heavy equipment and a gun truck. It was still pretty early in the war, so our vehicle lacked armor and its doors were made of soft canvas.

I settled into my seat. My vehicle didn't have air conditioning and it was so hot.

No one complained about the heat. We were trained to execute with whatever equipment we had and focus on the mission.

There were five of us inside the Humvee, including the driver and an open-air gunner in the back who could swivel around to shoot—it always reminded me of the hockey players in those stickman arcade games, the ones you could make twirl by twisting a knob, but a lot more dangerous.

By 0830 hours, we were finally set to go. Normally, I would sit up front next to the driver, but, this morning, I was placed behind the driver—this gave me a better vantage point for learning the route. There was one other soldier in the back with me: Lt. Woodard, my seatmate from the plane to Iraq. Between us was a big metal box that was packed with supplies, and it was crowded for us. We were now ready to leave our base. However humble it was, this was the moment when the base felt like a little sanctuary of safety in the middle of the desert.

Right before we left, a soldier came running up to my side of the Humvee.

"Ma'am, would you like me to take the door off?" he yelled over the sound of the engines. "I can put on a pedestal mount if you want."

When we were driving down the roads and the streets in Iraq, soldiers liked to have their weapons pointing out the window. A pedestal mount enabled you to keep your gun pointed out of the Humvee—it also made it easier to turn your body sideways and put your leg out while you held your gun. It wasn't a necessity, but it made the ride easier.

"Let's do it," I told the soldier without hesitation. Now I'd be like one of those stickman hockey guys.

We roared through the gate of the base, with dust and sand billowing in clouds all around us. It felt like it was getting hotter by the minute. I rested my left leg on the pedestal, pointing my weapon out. I felt safe. We were a line of ten vehicles full of highly trained personnel armed with M16 rifles. The soldier in the back of me was in a swivel pedestal with an M249 automatic weapon. We had the firepower and the manpower. I was a patriot with protection. Nothing was going to happen to me.

We drove in silence through the barren desert, the only sound that of the engines and the wind. The road was pretty deserted. Off in the distance, I could see little buildings and huts that were ordinary people's homes. It felt dirty, and the wind kicked up dust clouds that blocked out the increasingly angry sun. I was sweating like crazy, but we all were; we sweated so much that we barely noticed it.

The only person speaking was the officer in front, who was communicating with the other vehicles by walkie-talkie. Everyone was on the lookout for anything unusual or suspicious, and, if we saw anything, we would relay messages to all the vehicles trailing us.

It was business as usual. Ten vehicles on a routine supply convoy hoping for no trouble. Our part of the caravan scanned the road, watching.

About ten minutes in, we came upon a bridge. Army drivers were taught to always swerve when going under a bridge, in case someone is up on top and wants to drop an explosive—it makes for a more difficult target. Everything was done to enhance our chances of survival. This was the training.

I breathed in the desert air as our driver started to pull the wheel to swerve under the bridge.

And, as we made our way under the bridge, there was the loudest sound I had ever heard in my life.

Chapter 10

Wounded Soldier

It was deafening: *BOOM.*

An immediate cloud of black smoke. The acrid smell of explosives.

The driver swerved frantically to the left, and I looked up to see a crashed-in windshield. The female officer in the front seat was screaming: "IED! IED! We've hit an IED!"

Her voice rose with insistence, each syllable harder than the last.

We had hit a roadside bomb that had been on my side of the Humvee. The side without the door. The side with my left leg on the gun pedestal. The smell of burning metal was inescapable, growing stronger by the moment, strange and disturbing.

It felt like there was no time to process anything.

Our Humvee felt like it was in an endless state of whiplash. We slammed the left guardrail then ricocheted back in the other direction. The driver was furiously trying to regain control after going under the bridge, but the angle of our momentum was too violent after the explosion.

We crashed furiously into someone's home by the side of the road. Four Iraqis came running outside. The women were dressed in black from head to toe. In the chaos, it was impossible to tell what they were saying as they gesticulated and pointed. The soldiers in my vehicle got out and desperately began to surround the Humvee; we had been taught to protect at all costs the sensitive equipment it contained, including the computer electronics that could relay the location of all the American forces in the country.

I tried to step out of the vehicle to join them, but I couldn't unbuckle my seat belt. In all of the chaos, a bunch of heavy equipment had flown over to my side of the back seat, and the big heavy metal box was resting on my lap. *Convenient*, I thought.

I forced the buckle loose and twisted my body to try to get out. My eyes darted and fixed on a pool of sharp red blood amassing beneath me. I didn't know where it was coming from. There was so much of it. It was so bright. I knew something wasn't right.

"I'm hurt!" I screamed out.

Then I was gone. As soon as I screamed, I passed out. It was quick, probably only ten to fifteen seconds. It was the strangest experience. I went to the most beautiful, vibrant place, full of pink and purple flowers. It was the happiest, the most joyous place that I had ever experienced.

Then I resurfaced. Sergeant Pavich, a combat medic, was pulling me out of the vehicle by my bulletproof vest and laying me down on my back. He had been a few vehicles behind us and had heard my scream.

I had just been in the happiest place. Now I was trying to understand exactly where I was. It had been like a scene in the Beatles movie *Yellow Submarine,* where pretty music played, and everything was colorful and animated and full of life.

I'm in Iraq. I was on the ground. I was hurt.

Sergeant Pavich was working on me. He was desperately trying to start an IV in my arm, but it wasn't working. Lieutenant Woodard came around the opposite side of the vehicle.

"Oh my God!" he screamed when he saw me.

What? Why did he say that? What's so bad?

I was flat on my back and couldn't see my lower body. The pain hadn't set in yet. Things were moving fast and slow. There was a lot of commotion. I tried to move my foot, that seemed like the right thing to do. *There we go,* I thought as I moved it. *There it is. It hurts.*

Later, I would learn about phantom sensations: a common thing felt by people who were going through the experience of a traumatic amputation.

My orange bottle of Gatorade had flown out of the Humvee during the explosion and lay on the ground in front of me. I began to fixate on it. I stared at it, so close yet so far. I kept all my attention on the idea of quenching my thirst to keep from thinking about what was going on beneath my waist as they worked on me lying there on the road.

"I want a sip of that Gatorade," I said to anyone who moved within earshot of my raspy voice. "Pass it over here."

I was so thirsty. It was so hot, and I was lying on a boiling road in the desert thousands of miles away from home, and all I wanted was a sip of Orange Gatorade. But no one was willing to pass it to me. Why weren't they being loyal to a fellow soldier?

Sergeant Pavich wrapped my leg in a tourniquet to stop the bleeding. In that instant, I felt an overpowering rush of the most vicious pain imaginable.

Then I remembered our medical training. We had learned that, whenever a tourniquet is applied, it means that whatever is below it is no longer viable. That's when I realized that I was in a desperate situation.

People were shouting. The convoy commander was trying to get a hold of the Medivac helicopter so that I could be evacuated to the nearest military hospital. Maybe they would let me have a sip of Gatorade once I got there.

The frequency on the radio wasn't working, and she wasn't getting through. If she couldn't reach the helicopter, then the convoy commander had to go to Plan B. My fellow soldiers lifted me up, two on each side, and placed me on a stretcher. They carried me into the back of a five-ton pickup truck to take me to an aid station.

I was still on my back and still couldn't get a look at what was going on below my waist. I could see the soldiers trying not to stare, unable to hide their horrified expressions. So much blood. My uniform was torn to bits. They hastily applied another tourniquet.

"How bad is it?"

My left leg had just been blown off, and nobody wanted to tell me. The pain thickened and intensified as my leg dangled there. Another soldier joined me in the back of the pickup truck.

"Keep her awake!" someone yelled.

I focused my eyes to see who was with me—it was Lieutenant Woodard, who had sat next to me in the plane over to Iraq. Behind his glasses, I could see fear and worry in his eyes.

This definitely hadn't been among the possibilities we had talked about during that long plane ride.

"How about this weather?" the Lieutenant said to me. "Crazy over here, isn't it? Think the wind is going to pick up later? Hot, isn't it?"

He was talking fast, saying a lot of nothing. *The weather?* Yes, it was hot. Of course, it was hot. It was *always* hot here.

"Listen to me," I said. I spoke very deliberately over the sound of the truck engine.

"What is it?" Lieutenant Woodard asked.

"If I don't make it, tell my family that I love them."

The words came out without me really thinking about it. It seemed like the right thing to say in that moment. It was as though I had to say it.

The driver hopped in the front, another soldier jumped into the passenger seat and then we sped off. I was told that the nearest aid station was about ten minutes away. I jostled and bumped in the back of the truck, the hot dry wind rushing loud and the sun dancing in the sky as we sped along the road.

Usually, when a vehicle arrived at an aid station within an American base, it was required to stop for an identification check. Not today, when every second mattered. We tore through the gate without stopping.

"Wounded soldier!" I could hear the driver yelling. "Wounded soldier! Let us through! Let us through!"

Everyone was moving fast. I was hurried into an aid tent where a different set of medics adjusted my tourniquet and gave me morphine. They transferred me onto a different stretcher and then I was moving again, this time into the back of a helicopter.

My ears were filled with the roar of the helicopter engine as we rose off the ground and into the sky. We took off hard and banked, and my breath caught in my chest. Just a few seconds off the ground and I felt like I was falling out of the helicopter.

I had been in a helicopter a few times before. I remembered in that moment that I had actually gotten *married* in one. But this was different—there were no doors, and I could see the ground below as we banked sharply to the right, then just as sharply to the left. I really thought it was the end of me—wounded by a bomb, then tossed out of a moving helicopter.

About ten minutes passed. We leveled off, and I stared straight up from my stretcher. We started to lower down—coincidentally enough, into the Green Zone. Our convoy had been headed there, and, as it turned out, I got there first. Of all the ways I had imagined getting into the Green Zone, this hadn't been among them.

I was taken off the helicopter and put on a stretcher with wheels as someone sprinted me through a set of double doors. As I went through, someone yelled out.

"You're safe now," a voice was saying to me. "You're in an American hospital."

A soldier I didn't recognize appeared above me, sprinting by my side as I was carried into the American hospital. There were people there waiting to meet us, three or four of them as we sped through double doors that opened into a dimly lit hallway.

I was rushed into a room for surgery, doctors ripping off my uniform along the way. As I was wheeled into the operating room, something occurred to me.

"I need my Chapstick," I said. "Where's my Chapstick?"

That's all that occurred to me as I was being wheeled into surgery that would be needed to save my life—that little blue tube of Chapstick that I brought with me everywhere I went. I knew it was in one of the pockets of my uniform, even if I couldn't remember exactly which one. Just the thought of it was soothing, that blue color and the brand name on the label. It was something else to focus on other than what was happening to me.

I was in the operating room.

Then nothing.

I was waking up. There was a black letter "T" still on my forehead. Someone had written it there to stand for "tourniquet," so anyone who might come across me would know that I had been severely injured.

I looked over, and Dick was standing next to my bed. I couldn't think of how he had gotten there. He was always where he needed to be, and at the right time.

"I think I'm hurt," I told him. "I think something happened to my leg."

"Your leg is gone," he told me. "You don't have it anymore."

That is the story of the day Little Leg was born.

Chapter 11

On the Right Foot

A surgeon came into the room and handed me a cell phone, suggesting I call my parents. I felt so weak that it was difficult to dial their number. My mom answered after the first ring, sounding positive and cheerful. She knew that I had been bound on a convoy for the Green Zone and wanted to know how my adventure had gone.

I wasn't sure exactly what to say. The sound of her voice seemed to come from another place—the way things had been. She was light, funny, happy.

"Mom," I said softly. "Don't worry. Everything's going to be okay."

Even the silence on the line felt different now.

"Something bad happened to my leg," I said. "But I'm just really glad that it happened to me and not one of my soldiers."

Her happy tone shifted to panic as she started to reply. Dick grabbed the phone from my hand. I listened as he gave her the details: the convoy, the bomb, the rush to the hospital in the Green Zone. The fact that I didn't have my leg anymore.

"Don't let them take her leg! Don't let them do anything!" my mom cried out. "We're going to get her home and take her to the doctors here!"

I could hear my mom shouting into the phone, even though Dick was several feet away. She was hysterical. Of course, it was too late; my leg was already gone. The anguish in her voice—a mother whose daughter had just been gravely injured in war—it was a moment that felt pulled out of time, and I knew that it would haunt me for a long time to come.

I had just become the first female soldier to lose a limb in the Iraq War. This was a fact that I wouldn't be able to process right away. If there was a silver lining, it was that Dick had been able to reach my bedside while I was still in emergency surgery. When the roadside bomb went off, my commander contacted Dick's commander, and the Army got him to the hospital with incredible speed. I had my spouse there when I woke up, which was unheard of for a wounded soldier in Iraq.

When they rushed Dick to the Green Zone hospital, he only had partial information about the severity of my injury. When he got there, he had been afraid that I might already be dead. When he saw that I had only lost a leg, he was relieved. Sgt. Pavich had saved my life with that tourniquet by the side of the road.

Wounded soldiers in Iraq were taken to a major airbase in Balad, about fifty miles north of Baghdad. Everyone was flown out in order of whose situation was the most severe.

I was very high, pumped so full of morphine that I couldn't stop giggling. Dick was doing everything he could to keep me laughing, to keep me in a good mood.

"Remember that time we brought home that rotisserie chicken?" he asked.

I put my hand over my mouth and laughed out loud. "We sat outside our apartment," I replied. "We were so hungry we ate it all in the car before we even went inside."

That humor was a lifeline to me in those first hours. I'm sure I asked Dick for my blue Chapstick at some point—my mind kept returning to it—but he didn't have it.

Getting through those hours feels like a miracle now. At one point, we heard that distinct train whistle sound that meant rocket-propelled grenades were coming in.

We joked with each other: "At least we made it this far. Now we're going to get killed by incoming grenades while we're waiting for transport."

A couple of hours after my life-saving surgery, I was carted out of the holding room. That was a very short period of time, which spoke to how serious my injuries were. I kept laughing like a fool, though, and I wasn't sure of anything. I was in a fog of physical trauma, medication, and feelings that I'd never experienced before.

How I got to Balad is murky. It was probably by helicopter because it's too far to drive. I'd be returning to a part of Iraq where I had carried out missions when I first arrived—a few of those black ticks on the hat I had lost somewhere back by the roadside. This was a very different kind of mission than a transportation convoy, though—the mission was to stay alive.

* * *

The C-130 aircraft from Balad airbase to Landstuhl, Germany, was awfully silent, save for the sounds of IV bags being replaced and the moans of another soldier in pain. Soldiers were stacked three high—stretcher on top of stretcher on top of stretcher up and down the length of the military plane. We were the wounded ones, the ones who had escaped with our lives but were forever changed by the war zone. The place reeked of bandages and blood.

There was a wide assortment of injuries on board. Some soldiers had lost a limb from a bomb. Some had sustained traumatic gunshot wounds. Others had lighter injuries, like a broken ankle, and might end up returning to Iraq after they healed.

I was in a middle stretcher among dozens of other soldiers. There were still a ton of painkillers in my system, and I went in and out of consciousness; sometimes, things came into focus, other times, they seemed to bleed away. Dick had been given a seat across the aisle, but the chair was mostly empty—he spent most of the flight standing next to me. Along with the nurses who were on board, he tried to make sure I was as comfortable as I could be, given the circumstances.

By the time we reached Germany, the pain had returned—serious and tremendous amounts of pain. I was wheeled off the plane directly into my next surgery at Landstuhl's state-of-the-art military hospital.

That would be the first of four total surgeries I would endure over the next five days, as the doctors tried to get all the debris out of what remained of my leg. The nurses were in and out of my room so often that it might as well have had a revolving door. They kept administering the pain medications, furiously trying to keep up with my condition.

On the first night, Dick was taking some well-deserved sleep next to my bed. I opened my eyes to see a wounded soldier hobbling in on crutches, tearing back the sheet that divided my two-patient room in half.

It was Renina Miller, the soldier I'd done basic transportation corps with, the one whose name I had heard among the list of casualties earlier that week back at base. Now I was her injured roommate.

She came and stood by my bedside most of the night, struggling to balance on her crutches, holding my hand. I was in so much pain, and I was struggling to deal with it.

"You're going to be okay," she said, again and again, looking into my eyes.

The feel of her hand, the sound of her voice, her camaraderie helped me make it through that first night in the hospital. She demonstrated the true definition of what it means to be a soldier that night.

* * *

"My God, what happened?" shouted a familiar voice.

I woke up the next morning to my dad crying. He stared at the daughter he'd raised for twenty-four years and couldn't hold back the tears. I had just come out of a major operation and was lying in bed, phasing in and out of sleep, and, now that I came conscious, I was overwhelmed with pain.

Dad had been packing for a business trip to Vienna when he got the news and had frantically boarded a flight to be with me in Germany. His expression was terrible for me to see, alternating between a stunned stupor and flashes of panic— he clearly wanted to be strong, to take charge, to take care of me, but there wasn't much he could do. He kept sobbing and holding me, trying to catch his breath, in the worst state I'd ever seen him.

I tried to see myself through his eyes: bandaged up, IVs running in and out of my body, sheets covering my lower half, with one side normal and the other...an absence.

I knew I was fortunate to have a support system right away, something a lot of the other wounded soldiers didn't have. That same afternoon, my sister Amanda and her husband, Gavin, showed up at my door—it was a surprise, and I was shocked to see them. They were living in Slovakia at the time as youth missionaries, and they had gotten into a car and driven twelve hours to be with me. It gave me a rush of gratitude to have them there.

Time passed. I had lots of time. At that point, all I had was time. Time between doses of pain medications. Time between meals. Time between waking up and falling asleep again. Dad, Dick, Amanda, and Gavin all pitched in to sit with me and help make the time go by, playing card games and Scrabble. I was only left alone to go to the bathroom.

There were some moments of suffering. I had flashes of emotion. But they wouldn't let me wallow or sulk. They weren't going to throw me a pity party. "It is what it is," they told me more than once. "Let's just do what we need to do and move on."

It might have sounded like a cliché, but it was what I needed. Things started off, literally, on the right foot.

"Stay strong, you guys," I found myself saying when one of my people looked down. "We will get through this."

I found myself wanting to be a competitive player in the positivity chain. I kept thinking how much more difficult all of it would have been if I'd had to go it alone.

My mom was back home, but she was also doing her part. While my family was wheeling me around Landstuhl, doing everything they could to make me laugh, she was spending the week talking to every member of our extended family. She spent hours on the phone explaining what had happened, and the more she talked about it, the stronger she felt dealing with it.

Dick kept doing whatever he could to make me laugh. There was a big sign on the door of my room ordering visitors to wash their hands thoroughly before coming in, as I was at risk for infection. I was in my room a few days into my visit when I looked up to see that Dick had taken that command to the extreme. He was wearing a full set of hospital scrubs, a huge yellow surgical gown, a shower cap, and a mask. He looked like he was headed into surgery or entering some kind of disease zone that required a hazmat suit. For the next several days, I laughed about it whenever I thought about it—or whenever I needed a laugh.

He also helped me go to the bathroom, which was a major production in and of itself. There was a portable toilet next to my bed but getting to it was no easy feat. I was hooked up to a silver metal pole packed with IV bags and too many medications for me to count—I had to wheel it with me everywhere I went. Everything felt so awkward and difficult. Sometimes, when I made it all the way to the bathroom, it took so much effort that I would just sit there for a while, not wanting to go through the effort of the return journey. I was realizing how much I had taken for granted the smallest of things that I used to ask of my body.

* * *

By the third day in Landstuhl, I knew that it was time to get in touch with my friends back home and let them know what had happened. Dick pushed me in my wheelchair down the hall to a computer room full of big bulky desktop machines. With Dick's help, I typed an email to everyone on my contact list. It wasn't easy to concentrate but it needed to get done. I figured I could blame all the typos on the morphine:

Subject: not such good news

Hey everyone. Unfortunately, this message is not good news, so brace yourself for a bit of bad news. on 13APR I was driving in a convoy to the Green Zone, as they call it from Taji. I was riding along learning the route in a HUMV that had no doors. We were about halfway there and we hit an IED (improved explosive device) on the other side of the behicle as we passes under a bridge. This caused the drived to swerve and we hit 2 guardrails before hitting someone's house. Becasue my leg was outside the vehicle it hit both guardrails as we went by and pretty much ruined it. I was rushed to a field hospital where I was soon after medevaced. I lost my left foot immediately and all the skin below my knee was torn off. They put a torniquet on and in order to save my life they had to amputate my leg below the knee. I had lost a lot of blood and recieced 4 unts of blood- I was flown to Balad, where we stayed until I was flown to Germany, where I am now. Since I've been here. I have had another surgery where they cleaned out my wound. Good news is there is little to no dead tyissue meaning that they won't have to amputate anymore, however, I have a fractured femur which causes quite a bit of pain whenever moved. I have to wait until the fracture is healed before putting any pressure on a 'new' leg.

I see myslef as being exteremely lucky as I could be kia right now instead of just missing a leg. My husband gets to come back to the states with me, and both my sister, brother-in-law and my dad are all out here visiting right now. I should be flying out of here within the next few days to Walter Reed hospital in Washington DC. Apparently, they specialize on amputees and I will get a leg that will manueveur just as my real leg would have.

Let me just tell you i don't think it has all set in. It still feels like I can move my toes, my foot, but it is not there. It was definitely one of the most painful things I have ever been through, but feel very lucky that nothing more happened. I have had so much support here. and I know things will only get better. I am assuming I will be discharged from the Army as soon as I get back. I am assuring myself that I will be up and doing things I have always done as soon as possible. Dick and I still have big dreams and WILL still climb mountains, fly airplanes, etc. He has been so wonderful to me...let's hope he doesn't have to go back to Iraq.

SO. there's no need to send anymore mail- I will not be headed back there again. I will keep the updates coming- and if anyone is in the DC area I know I will be there for quite some time getting my new leg put into place.

Hope to hear from you soon
Melissa

It was the best I could do at the time. Looking back, it was obvious from the email that I wasn't in too bad of a place mentally at the time. It could have been so much worse. The morphine played a major role in managing the physical pain. You also can't overstate the power of simply being grateful to be alive. I was straining so hard to stay positive. Somehow, I thought, if I could lift the spirits of the people who cared about me and were worried about me, maybe I would also heal faster.

I was also under no illusions about the road ahead of me. It was going to be long and bumpy. I remembered seeing amputees when I was growing up, whether it was in person or on TV. I'd always felt compassion for them and wondered what their lives were like. I had never known anyone who had lost a limb, but I remembered thinking, *Oh, that poor person* when I'd see someone in a wheelchair or using a prosthetic limb.

It's ironic, because starting then and continuing to today, that's the exact sentiment that I don't want people feeling for me. Today, I see an amputee and all I can see is the amazing things they're capable of, and all the ways that their life is great. Earlier in life, I realized, I hadn't seen them entirely as persons apart from the amputation. Now I wonder if they're married, what their job is, what their life story might be like. There's no need to feel any pity or sorrow for someone who has a disability. There's no reason to say, *That poor person* because they're just like us. And we're just like them—just people.

My fellow soldiers in Iraq had been told what had happened, hearing the news from the platoon leaders when I didn't make it back to camp from the convoy. It wasn't unusual to hear reports of vehicles getting hit by IEDs, although it was rare to hear about a fellow soldier losing a limb. I'd later learn that the news of my injury alarmed and disturbed some of my comrades back at the base, so much so that a few of them were taken off duty for a week to reset.

There was a phone by the nightstand of my hospital bed in Landstuhl, though it was silent until the third day when it finally rang. I gingerly reached for it, just stretching from my pillow causing me pain. To my surprise, it was Captain Vogel calling me from Iraq.

"I'm so sorry," I said again and again before he could get anything out of his mouth after his name. "I'm so sorry."

I felt so guilty, safe in a decent bed, warm, with decent food and temperature-controlled comfort while my soldiers were under that blazing sun, in harm's way every single minute of the day.

"And how can I replace my walkie-talkie?" I asked him, knowing that the device that had been issued to me by the Army, and which was lost in the attack, was considered sensitive equipment.

"There's no need to apologize," Captain Vogel said calmly. "I should be the one saying I'm sorry."

After five days in Landstuhl, I was stable enough to head home to the safe haven of the United States. I started counting down the minutes, knowing how much it would bolster my strength to be back home again. The Army allowed Dick to come to Walter Reed National Military Medical Center in Washington with me, with the presumption that he would eventually have to return to the war in Iraq.

Dick and I boarded another C-130 stacked with wounded soldiers, headed to DC where the severely wounded from Iraq and Afghanistan were taken. I knew that my mom was going to be meeting me there, which made me even more impatient to touch down on the other side of the Atlantic. I imagined being in her arms, replaying our first hug since my injury over and over again my mind. I needed her comforting embrace more than ever.

This flight was even longer than the one from Iraq to Germany, and I was lying down on the top stretcher, surrounded again by other wounded soldiers. There is nothing in the world like military camaraderie, and the nurses on that flight worked nonstop to try to make us all as comfortable as possible. The poor soldier next to my stretcher had an IV in his neck, and he kept staring at me as Dick passed me a Gatorade bottle to quench my thirst. (Years later, that soldier—his name is Joe Bowser—would become a dear friend. I'd learn then that all he'd wanted to do on that flight was work up enough strength to ask for a sip of my Gatorade—just like me days earlier, when I'd been injured by the roadside bomb. Now Joe and I celebrate our "alive days"—the birth of our new lives after our injuries— one day apart from each other.)

We landed at Andrews Air Force base near Walter Reed in the middle of the night. It turned out it was common practice for a large aircraft filled with wounded soldiers to land under cover of night, to avoid photos and press coverage.

It felt like my heart returned to a familiar beat, just knowing that I was on home soil again. But, as usual, my experience changed from hour to hour—now I felt mentally locked into a state of confusion. Our bus to Walter Reed contained about a dozen soldiers. It was pitch black outside, and I winced in newly intensified pain whenever we hit a bump in the road. There were other soldiers around me doing the same, moaning at the same moments in the drive. I was amazed at how painful it all was.

Where did the morphine go? I found myself wondering. *Don't they know I just lost my leg?*

We finally pulled up by the fountain in the big circular drive in front of Walter Reed. Even at night, it was an impressive building, all brick and white columns in front with countless windows looking down. The bright hospital lights nearly blinded us all after sitting in the dark for so long—figuratively as well as literally, because none of us knew what came next.

I was put on a stretcher and wheeled into the hospital that was going to be my home for the next three months. I lost my leg on April 13 and got to Walter Reed on April 20.

The week in between, I was coming to fully understand, was one of the toughest of my entire life. I got through it with help from my family, from the doctors and nurses, and from the morphine. I was getting a glance at my second chance at life.

I had spotted a glimmer of hope in all of it, in me. Even if I experienced a second of pure optimism, I would cling to it. I'd try to make it happen again. Resurfacing gradually from the painkillers, I had begun to realize and accept that I had lost a leg—and nothing more.

I was one of the lucky ones.

Chapter 12

Back on Home Soil

When I woke up my first morning at Walter Reed, Dick and my mom were there beside me. Otherwise, I had the room all to myself—I had gotten extremely lucky to have a private room, with a bed, a nightstand, a chair, and even a private bathroom. I was moving up in the world. This was even an upgrade over my little private trailer in Iraq. Most of the other soldiers shared the kind of double room with a sheet down the middle dividing it that I'd had in Landstuhl.

Part of the reason for my upgrade in accommodations, maybe even the entire reason, was because I was the only wounded female soldier there. The hospital staff kept reminding me that I was part of history, which was something that I more or less ignored at that point because I was so fixated on my missing leg.

I had more surgeries in those early days at Walter Reed, going in and out of anesthesia and still being given pain killers.

Things were fuzzy. Nurses were constantly coming and going, cleaning my wound and changing the heavy bandages around my leg.

At that point, I still didn't look down there while the bandages were being changed. I was afraid of what I'd see. I preferred staying still as a mummy, even when I was in agony from being moved or having the bandages pulled off, rather than looking down and seeing the stump that remained of my leg.

Maybe none of it was true, I would think sometimes. Maybe I still had my leg. Maybe it was all a bad dream that I was going to wake up from any minute.

Dream or not, I wasn't taking chances. I got alarmed and upset by the very idea of throwing a quick glance below my knee.

In between the nurses coming in and out, I would sleep. The staff had provided me with a pain pump that I could push every hour, which would dispense more medication through the seemingly permanent IV connected to my arm. I had a timer on my watch set to go off every hour, and, each time it sounded, I pushed the pump's tiny black button, feeling a release deep inside my body.

Ahhhh. Yes. That's the stuff.

I couldn't wait to push that pump again and again. I wasn't able to move around much because I had a fracture in what was left of my femur, the biggest bone in the human body. It was covered up by a pressurizing contraption called an external fixator, with pins in each part of the bone trying to push the bone back in place, which hurt. A lot.

My temporary home was Ward 57, which was where they initially brought all the severely wounded soldiers from Iraq and Afghanistan. I had no idea how many others were in there with me, but I sensed that it was a lot. When I was able to take my first trip down the hallway in my wheelchair, I looked in rooms to my left and my right as I rolled down the hall, amazed by how many other soldiers were there who had lost their eyesight, both their arms, both their legs or even three limbs. War is merciless. I was surrounded by dozens of other soldiers who had gone through similar traumatic experiences while fighting for and serving our country. Things we had never imagined in our lives had happened to all of us, and so quickly that we hardly had time to process or understand them. We were just *there*.

Several of my friends flew in to join Dick and my parents during my first weekend at Walter Reed. All of them had pretty much dropped everything to come to support me and be by my side. My friend, Missy, who was going to law school at American University in Washington, was able to provide everyone with a place to stay—even if that meant some of them slept on the floor.

I was suddenly surrounded by comrades, loved ones, family and friends. So many of the other wounded soldiers there were on their own. I was so thankful to be encircled by so many people dear to me. That love, that comfort, and those hugs—their importance can't be overestimated for someone dealing with so much physical pain and emotional loss.

We couldn't fit everyone in my room, so we would commandeer a lounge in the hospital and spend hours together. They held my hand and cracked joke after joke, keeping my spirits afloat, even when I was feeling weak and hazy. There was a lot of laughing. There was also some crying. I found myself trying hard to put on a brave face for everyone, gritting my teeth and trying to laugh even when the pain in my leg was burning. I wanted to make it seem like what I was going through was perfectly normal, totally manageable.

I'd often have to wheel back to my room to be alone when I got too tired or when the pain felt overwhelming. I felt that acting brave was part of getting through this. And I'm not one to agonize over my wounds in front of others.

* * *

One afternoon that week, we had several of us gathered in my room for a group photo, with everyone arranged around me on my bed. Just as we were shooting the picture we were startled by a loud knock at the door.

We looked up, and standing there was the famous actress Susan Sarandon, who had starred in *Thelma & Louise*. She looked surprised to have stumbled upon a room packed wall to wall with visitors, and we were all startled as we realized who she was. What was this famous person doing at *my* hospital, outside *my* door? It was so strange—I had an Academy Award-winning movie star right in front of me, at what was the lowest point in my life.

She came into the room to chat with us for a little while before moving on down the hall to meet other wounded soldiers. I would quickly learn that celebrities, politicians, and high-ranking military officers often visit patients at Walter Reed. This was a cool thing that everyone appreciated in their own way, a way to create moments that pulled us away from the reality of recovering from a life-changing injury.

I thought if a big part of my body was going to be wrapped up like a mummy, with me going in and out of operating rooms, at least I was going to meet some celebrities in this place.

I'd get to meet Tom Hanks, Sean Astin, Donald Rumsfeld and his wife Joyce, Ozzy and Sharon Osbourne, and others. It still felt as though I was in a dream sometimes, although these were more like nice dreams than nightmares.

Tom Hanks was one of my favorites, a truly nice guy. Later, he would come to an event I attended and wave at me from the audience—he has a way of making people feel special, myself included.

Ozzy Osbourne was pretty much the same in person as who you see on TV. He wandered aimlessly around my room while he was visiting me, while Sharon sat on my bed and kept me company with small talk to pass the time. All of these famous people were polite and respectful. They would thank soldiers for their service and sacrifice, and they graciously reminded us that what we had done for our country mattered. It helped remind soldiers that there was a purpose to what had happened to them and that they were appreciated.

* * *

The nights at Walter Reed were the worst times. That's when the doubts would come.

My family and friends would be back at Missy's or their hotel rooms. The sky was black, and the bustle of the day settled to quiet. I couldn't sleep.

There was nothing else to think about than the reality that I had lost my leg.

It wasn't really a matter of feeling sorry for myself most of the time. It was more of a deep sense of questioning the future.

What was it going to be like to try to walk again? Would I be able to run? Would I be independent again? What was my new life going to be like? I really had no idea.

I knew that I needed to start deciphering what the new normal was going to be for me—even through the pain and the medication this was increasingly clear. I was only twenty-four years old, after all. I had a lot of years left.

One night, all of those thoughts were swirling, and it was enough to feel overwhelmed. It was hard to picture the future, but I realized at once that I'd be able to fill in the blanks. The main thing was that I had the power inside me to make a crucial choice—how I was going to approach the future.

So many of the other wounded soldiers were worse off than me. Every single one of them was going to have to dig inside for the strength and belief to make the most of what they still had. For me, I had three good, healthy limbs. I had my eyesight and my heart was beating strong. And I was alive. I was still here.

That was the first moment since the IED went off that I looked at myself long and hard in the mirror. I was still me.

I couldn't feel sorry for myself. I thought of hurling through the neighborhood on Sweet Thunder, the wind on my face and the trees whizzing past. I thought of tumbling on the gymnastics mat, meeting the challenges and limits of my body head-on. I remembered the power of my patriotism and belief when I signed up for the Army.

There was sadness. There was doubt. But these are things everyone has, at one time or another, no matter what life gives them or takes away. From that point forward, I tried to remember that the greatest power is in choosing what to make of life. I would feel sadness and pain, but I could still fight through it. I could try to smile. I could feel the wind of adventure and make the most of what I had in any situation.

Chapter 13

First Steps: Pride, Patriotism, Country Music

My mom stayed with me for an entire month at Walter Reed while my dad was in and out between work trips; just like when I was in Iraq, I didn't want my mom to worry, and often I would force a smile so that I didn't seem angry, bitter, or sad in front of her. Only once did I crack and show her my tears. Mom was sitting beside me in bed when a nurse came to check-in. After the nurse had completed her routine and left, I broke down.

I was like a river dam that had suddenly burst. I was crying uncontrollably.

"That nurse has no idea how lucky she is to have both her legs," I said, my face messy with tears.

She took me in a consoling, much-needed mother-daughter hug. That was the hug I had fantasized about while waiting in the phone line in Iraq, and the one I'd needed every day since I got back to the United States. As my mom released me, I battled away the tears. Life was still happening.

We had a welcome turn when Dick was able to stay permanently with me in the U.S., living in the Mologne House—a hotel next to the hospital reserved for the families of wounded soldiers. High-ranking military officers at Walter Reed had agreed to process the paperwork that allowed him to stay by my side. He was going to be stationed in Washington and assigned to a military unit called the Old Guard, a name for the Army's 3rd Infantry Regiment whose primary mission is to march in ceremonies and military funerals. The soldiers in Dick's new unit were the ones who guarded the Tomb of the Unknown Soldier and marched in presidential inaugurations. Dick would even end up participating in Present George W. Bush's second-term inauguration. It was a pretty lenient assignment, and he had a schedule that enabled him to be at the hospital most days while I slowly recovered. We wouldn't need those walkie-talkies anymore, listening for them to squawk so we could steal a moment to communicate.

I was improving mentally, but I still wasn't permitted outside the hospital walls for several more weeks because of my low white blood cell count; the doctors would worry I would be prone to an infection and that my condition would worsen if I ventured out in public. I had a whiteboard on the wall of my room where my blood count was posted—we would have a mini celebration every time it went up, even by a miniscule amount. I was learning how the smallest victories, even over things that used to be completely taken for granted, were now substantial achievements.

Slogging in and out of surgeries, waiting for my deep row of stitches—a suture line—to heal, so that I could be fitted with a prosthetic leg was grueling and slow. I was finding out that even a traumatic injury wasn't improving my skills at being patient.

* * *

The President came to visit the hospital, but I missed him. I had been granted permission to leave the hospital and attend my grandfather's funeral. I hadn't been especially close to him, but it was a difficult day for my family—we all knew how much my grandfather had impacted my dad, and this was a hard time for him. He was visibly upset, and, other than that day in Landstuhl, it was one of the few times in my life that I had seen him moved to tears.

It was also the first time I had left Walter Reed since coming back to the United States. I was still on pain medications and my temporary release came with a lot of precautions. Dick was familiar with the daily ins and outs of my treatment, and he was able to convince the hospital that it wasn't necessary to send a doctor or a nurse to travel with us. My mom and dad drove us nearly a thousand miles to Ohio for the funeral. I attended the service on crutches, my arm connected to an IV that supplied medications on the hour.

At the reception, I started to feel faint. I made my way back to the car on my crutches and laid down on some pillows in the back seat. I tenderly placed the IV bar on a car door handle. I thought of how I looked: at my grandfather's funeral, strung out in the back seat of my dad's car on strong pain medication, unable to walk. I stung with embarrassment. Everyone else was leading their lives, paying their respects, and I couldn't even stand up properly. I wished that I could have done more to help my dad on one of the most difficult days of his life.

* * *

Two months into my stay at Walter Reed, my suture line had healed. I was able to be fitted for my first prosthetic leg. There was a lab at Walter Reed where all the prosthetics were built, and it never lacked for people—it was a hangout place for many soldiers. The whir of the drum sanders and the whine of the band saws signaled hope for many of the soldiers, the sound of taking back some sense of normality. The lab was the place to be between therapy sessions and doctor's appointments— anything so that wounded soldiers didn't have to sit alone in their rooms staring at the walls.

I found that it helped me to keep my mind occupied by getting involved more than most in the process of fitting my prosthetic leg. The lab staff allowed me to visit often, poking my nose around their work and prodding the arms and legs being crafted there.

The prosthetist-amputee relationship is very intimate—they have to get all up in your business to make sure the prosthetic fits comfortably and works optimally. There's really no room for shame in it from either side. My prosthetist, Dennis, would fit my leg tightly with a shrinker—a piece of material similar to a compression sock, which was designed to remove fluids and relieve swelling. I'd started to wear it all day and night, and, once the fluid was suitably reduced, I was cast for my first leg using plaster and fiberglass.

It's a similar process to creating a cast for a broken arm or foot—with the main difference being that the mold is removed immediately from the body part as soon as it hardens. As soon as Dennis removed the cast from my leg, the result was a mold that would become my socket—cupped around the bottom of my residual limb above where my knee once used to be. It was a big step forward, and worth the pain.

Fifty-two days had passed after I lost my leg when I was gifted with a new one.

"Here's your leg," Dennis said to me, almost too nonchalantly, as he handed me a new "leg" composed of the socket, a long piece of titanium where the knee would go, and a foot that looked nothing like my own. "You're going to walk with this today."

I did a double-take. It was surreal. Was he really talking to me? Was I really going to be able to stand up for the first time in months?

It was a strange and unfamiliar feeling settling into the socket, the first time I felt my flesh and the augmenting device come into contact in a way that truly meant business. My limb was being held by a clear bucket, attached to a pole that was linked to an artificial foot.

"Okay. Stand up and try taking a few steps," Dennis said. He pulled me up to a set of parallel bars for assistance.

"What do you mean, take a few steps?" I asked him "How am I supposed to walk with this thing?"

It was a moment of frustration. Out of the corner of my eye, I then caught a glimpse of another patient on the other side of the physical therapy gym. He was moving with a walker. He was missing both of his legs and an arm. I had to get real with myself. If he was on his feet and moving while missing three limbs, then I didn't have much of an excuse.

I slowly set my good foot on the ground, and then the prosthetic one. I was hanging onto the parallel bars for dear life.

Those singing cadences from Army training came in handy at a time like this. *Left*. Wait a few seconds. *Right*. A couple more seconds. *Left*. *C'mon, you can do it, Melissa*. A couple seconds. *Right*. *Left*.

I was smiling wider than I had in a long time. There was pain, but I didn't really feel it—I was just so excited to be standing and moving again.

"Take it easy; don't be on your feet for too long," Dennis and my physical therapist Bob warned me. "You get ten minutes on the parallel bars."

I knew they were right—my body needed to ease into the socket and adjust to the prosthetic leg. But I was so excited, and I kept going and going. Dennis finally forced me to stop, so that I could give my body some rest.

That was going to be my recovery process in a nutshell: me pushing, and nearly begging the hospital staff to teach me the next step and get me going.

* * *

From there, it got better and better. I woke up every day determined to take even more steps than I had the day before. I learned to put my leg on by myself, and to keep moving, even if I sometimes needed crutches or a cane. More and more, I would walk without an assistive device, which was a huge victory every time. It felt real: I was finally going to regain my independence.

I still hadn't looked at myself in the mirror much without my leg, but I had started to more frequently. I liked what I saw: me standing on two legs again. I kept returning to Dennis to be fitted for new sockets as my leg continued to shrink. Today, I've cycled through dozens of sockets, but I've always held on to that first one.

The camaraderie among the soldiers at Walter Reed was as strong as that on the battlefield, and, as my stay there went on, my fellow wounded soldiers became like family. We felt that we were all in it together, and we tried to be around to encourage each other taking our first steps or cheering on milestones in one another's recoveries. Pretty soon, a second wounded female soldier had joined me on Ward 57, then a third, then a fourth.

Danielle Greene had lost her arm below the elbow. Dawn Halfaker lost her arm at the shoulder. Tammy Duckworth was missing one leg above the knee, the other below the knee, and had sustained a serious injury to one of her arms. I was now surrounded by three other strong, battle-tested women, and we immediately banded together without even thinking about it. I was moving around more fluidly by the day, moving pretty fast with a walker, and I was able to show them my leg and explain the first steps in using a prosthetic to regain independence.

I was able to leave the hospital more frequently now, looking forward with anticipation to Friday nights when some of us wounded soldiers could leave Walter Reed for a delicious dinner put on at Fran O'Brien's Steakhouse. I didn't want to complain about the hospital food, but *that* was a delicious break. And, everywhere we went, people thanked us for our service and gave us VIP treatment.

We were taken for a visit to the Capitol on the Fourth of July and made to feel like rock stars. We had an elegant dinner, and an amazing concert with country music (my favorite) featuring Brad Paisley, and then a spectacular fireworks display that we cheered on from the Capitol's balcony.

In my mind, we all happened to be in the wrong place at the wrong time when we got injured. But so many people were glorifying our service, with gifts and flags and books and clothes. We were almost like celebrities in our own right. It also helped make us feel that love of country is bigger than any one individual—that pride, duty, and patriotism were what was being honored more than any of us as a single person. Still, it never got old.

Chapter 14

Finding a New Purpose

Everything seemed to be going as well as it possibly could. I had learned to walk again. I had regained so much confidence, and my discharge from the hospital was approaching.

There was just a routine procedure before I was allowed to leave: a standard MRI to ensure that proper healing had taken place. It wasn't supposed to be a big deal.

For me, what they discovered was a very big deal—an infection that had traveled six inches up the bone of what remained of my femur.

Instead of being discharged, I was sent straight to surgery where six additional inches had to be removed from what was left of my leg. *Six inches.* Almost as long as a dollar bill. That is quite a lot when you're already missing part of a limb. Every inch matters because the more leg you have, the more stability you have to work with. More bone means more ease of movement.

When I first lost my leg, it was right above the knee. Now it would go even higher. As the news washed over me, I felt like I couldn't catch a break. It sucked.

But that day, just like on April 13, I had no choice. I couldn't tell the infection to go away. I couldn't refuse to go back into the operating room. The doctors said that, if the operation wasn't performed right away, the infection was going to travel even higher up the bone.

I took deep breaths. I wiped away the tears. I thought about everything I had learned about focusing on what I could control and accept what was given and what I couldn't change.

All I could control was how I responded.

* * *

I had already gone through the recovery process from a major surgery. That helped. I knew what to expect, step by step, and, since it was the second time around, I was confident that we could fast-track the whole process.

Three months and fifteen surgeries after arriving at Walter Reed, my suture line had healed again. I was cast for a new socket, and I learned how to re-walk for the second time. I dealt with the pain, the slow healing. I tried to keep a sense of humor. I focused on choosing to stay positive as much as I could. And, for the second time, I was given that routine MRI.

This time, I passed.

I pushed myself from Walter Reed to the Mologne House next door, where I would live with Dick for a few weeks while continuing my rehab. Dick had to help with the whole under-taking of leaving the hospital because I had collected so many photos, and so many gifts and packages, that I could barely see over the top of the pile. I needed his help in getting to our new home, and I still had a lot of work to do. But I finally had the sense that the worst was over.

I desperately longed to feel normal again. That meant living my life off the hospital grounds and figuring out all of the details of living my life on my own. Many wounded soldiers end up staying at Mologne House for the entire course of their rehab, which, for some, can last more than a year. I wanted to break free of the hold of Walter Reed, and Dick and I searched for a rental house someplace nearby, along with Missy, who had just broken up with her boyfriend and was going through a period of emotional turmoil herself.

The first time I completely left the Walter Reed campus on my own, without an IV or any hospital staff, was when I went with Dick and Missy on a fifteen-minute drive to check out a rental house we were fairly sure we wanted. I sat in the backseat with the window down, listening to the country music turned up on the car stereo.

I felt so alive.

We were right about the house, and we ended up putting down a deposit to rent it.

I wasn't going to live in a hospital again. I was going to be able to get around on my own.

I was going to be free.

* * *

Early in the Iraq War, it was uncommon for amputees to remain in the Army after being wounded. Years later, many amputees would not only remain on active duty but return to combat with their prosthetic legs. For those wounded early on in the war, however, this wasn't the case, and many amputees, especially those with amputations as high as mine, were told they would be given a desk job if they remained in the Army.

The last thing I wanted to do now that I was up and moving was to sit down at a desk, even if it meant serving in the military for the country that I loved so much. Every bone in my body, including the ones in my prosthesis, was telling me not to sit still. So, after I moved into the rental house with Dick and Missy, I chose to take medical retirement from the military, to move on with my life and see what I could do next. Of course, my original plan had been to stay in the military for a few more years—so what *did* come next? This was clearly going to be a new phase of my life, but there was no plan for me.

Five days a week, I would still drive to Walter Reed for physical therapy, occupational therapy, and to work on my prosthetic leg. That was all about as entertaining as it sounds. More and more, I needed something else in my life to keep me going, to pass the time, to keep me engaged—most of all, I didn't want to be sitting around the house and dwelling on everything that had happened. The blood, the IVs, the tourniquets: I really needed to keep my mind off all that. But, with Missy and Dick both gone for most of the day and with my schedule pretty much completely open other than appointments at Walter Reed, I was alone.

Downtime—never my strong suit. Waking up in the house every day, trying to figure out what I was going to do to fill the house—that was a challenge in itself. Should I rearrange the bookshelf? Should I go through all my clothes and see what still fits? Should I just get out and try to see how far I could walk?

I love being busy. I love being around people, and activity. I didn't want my only daily adventure or achievement to be a fifteen-minute drive to and from Walter Reed. I needed a bigger world. And even those trips to the hospital were becoming less and less frequent, less and less necessary. I wanted a normal life. I wanted to be that Melissa I remembered my parents telling me I could be: strong, independent, making her own choices and expressing her own will.

A park district magazine came in the mail, and I leafed through it until a neighborhood painting class caught my eye. I signed up for it. Because I was still recovering from my last surgery, which had, in reality, been another amputation, it was a big effort for me to park my car and walk down the street to where the classes were held. It turned out that I was going to be the youngest by far in the art class, and the older ladies there were exceedingly kind to me.

The class lasted six weeks, and they all learned my story. After all, anyone would be curious. So there I was, a woman who just lost her leg in a war taking a neighborhood painting class with ten old ladies. I wasn't sure if they had affection for me, or just found me funny. It didn't matter to me. My favorite painting that I made in the class—a bear in the woods—is framed and still hanging in my parents' house today. Every time I look at it, I think about little victories and how important they can be.

It was this class that helped wake me up to how exploring creativity was going to be one of the ways I found meaning and purpose in my new life. I had to tie my restlessness into my new life and my reason to live.

I realized how fascinated I was by how I was fit for my prosthetic leg—and I imagined how rewarding it must have been for Dennis to watch me literally standing on my own two feet for the first time in my new life. It must have been incredible to be so instrumental in such an important moment, and

I fancied seeing the whole thing taking place from his point of view. That's when I decided I would go back to school and study the art of prosthetics.

I hadn't even known that the field existed until I needed my new leg, and now it felt like a strong purpose to learn how to help others remake their lives the same way I was trying to refashion my own. Before I could apply for prosthetics school, though, I had to complete some prerequisite courses in physics and anatomy that hadn't been required for my undergrad degree in Communications. It also solved my problem of needing something to fill my days when I signed up for classes at the University of Maryland-Rockford, a community college close to Walter Reed—it moved me outside that circle of doctor's appointments to the quiet house, expanding my life.

Science was never my strong suit, and I was still attempting to walk independently with my prosthetic leg—so I wasn't exactly at the top of my game when I returned to school as a twenty-four-year-old. I aimed to earn at least a B or a C in my classes, to keep improving with my walking every day, and to find a way to fit in. I think it was obvious to my professors and my fellow students that I was struggling sometimes. Sitting on hard benches in class with the wood bumping against my prosthetic leg was painful and distracting—it seemed that every physical situation presented some kind of new challenge that I needed to face and figure out.

"Just curious, were you in the war?" my physics teacher asked me. "How did you lose your leg?"

It was the final day of class. I gave him the short version of what had happened, and, as though by some magic, I received an A-minus. I blinked, unsure for the moment if he felt sorry for me or if I had really earned a grade higher than I thought I could pull off. I took a minute, then decided not to question things. I took the A-minus and moved on; if it was a token of appreciation, I was going to accept it.

Chapter 15

Back in the Water

I decided it was time to get back to my roots. Just like in college, I started waking Missy up at five in the morning on the dot (not that I would have necessarily chosen that early hour, but Missy was in law school and we had to get our workout in before her daily classes started) to come swim with me twice a week at the Bethesda Naval Center pool. I wanted to get back into athletics and swimming beckoned because it didn't require me to wear my prosthetic leg.

This was a new challenge: I had to use my crutches to make my way onto the pool deck, being extra careful not to slip and hurt myself on the wet tiles.

The first time was a highly self-conscious experience. I moved slowly, smelling that familiar chlorine and hearing the echoing splashes of the lane swimmers who had come for early morning workouts. I looked around. No one was staring, at least not obviously.

I got in the water. I had anticipated that moving in the pool would feel noticeably different—swimming with one leg—though when I imagined it the night before, I had been totally unsure what to expect. But, once I got in, it felt completely normal. In fact, as the familiar buoyant sensation of floating came over me, it was like gravity had let go and I was able to forget that I was even missing the leg. It took my mind off it, and I was able to feel completely whole again while I was in the water.

Whole. Alive. Accepted.

There in the pool, I suddenly remembered what it felt like to be like everybody else. Like a competitor, able to push against boundaries and feel the exhilaration of muscles and mind working together.

Pretty soon, all the morning swimmers at the Bethesda pool knew who I was, and all my nerves dissolved. Sometimes curious people who meant well would ask me (and often still do) why I didn't swim in circles—like I was missing a propeller on a boat rather than a leg. I usually stifled a chuckle as I explained that swimming is mostly an upper-body sport and that I had no problems swimming in a straight line.

Pushing through the water, the rhythm of the strokes, timing my breathing, feeling my muscles respond and the rush of motion: I couldn't get enough of any of it. Pretty soon, even if Missy was too tired to wake up at five, I would head over and swim alone. I was in my element for the first time in quite a while.

* * *

As the months went on, I went over to Walter Reed less and less. One day, when I was there for an appointment, I checked a bulletin board on the wall where there were announcements for activities and opportunities for wounded vets.

I stopped and took a long look at a sign-up sheet. It was for the New York City Marathon, where participants could use a handcycle. This was with a nonprofit called Achilles International, whose mission was to empower people with disabilities to participate in mainstream sporting events.

Things were changing inside me as a result of all that early morning swimming. My drive, my need for challenge was sparked to the extent that, looking at that sign-up sheet, I knew that I wasn't going to truly be myself again until I returned to sports.

I signed up, not even knowing what it would entail.

Every Tuesday afternoon, I started riding a borrowed handcycle to ride on the trails outside the hospital. I had a lot of work to do, and quickly, to prepare for the marathon. The race was in November, and it was August already.

Together with some other soldiers, I learned to power a bike with my arms as a member of the Achilles Freedom Team. It was hard work, and it made my arms sore for days afterwards, but the rush of speed felt like returning to worlds I knew as far back as my childhood. The other riders and I would brag to each other about how many miles we had trained in a given day, not really fully comprehending the enormity of cycling the full 26.2 miles that a marathon requires. During these Achilles practices, something else fortunate happened—I met someone close to my age named Keri who would play a major part in my life years later.

For me and the other soldiers, it was so sweet to have a goal. It was a giant step toward normalcy, striving for something outside the hospital walls. I'd never endured propelling myself through 26.2 miles of anything in my life, though, and the furthest I made it on the handcycle in my training was a long ride of fifteen miles. It was unexpected that the New York City Marathon was going to bring me back into my athletic comfort zone.

* * *

When the first Sunday in November finally arrived, I figured that I would be nervous as heck, but the reality was the opposite.

I was surrounded by a sea of thousands of jazzed-up people at the starting line in Staten Island. It felt like a holiday, a celebration, and there were dozens of other wounded vets nearby—many of whom I had practiced with weekly. We waved, we said hello, we offered words of encouragement: *You got this.* My heart soared. The energy at the starting line electric.

Of course, the other vets gave me a sense of a powerful purpose. This was the first athletic competition I'd braved since losing my leg, and it was huge—a world-class race with people from all over the world. I would be racing through the five boroughs of New York with people who looked just like me, who had fought the same battles to be here, who were all digging deep inside. I loved it.

I had a blue handwritten sign on the back of my handcycle that read: *27th Main Support Battalion Bravo Company Come Home Safely.*

The race grew near. At the starting line on the Verrazzano Bridge, one of the seasoned handcyclists came over to me.

"Now don't start out too hard," he cautioned me. "You want to have enough energy at the end to finish."

"Okay, sure," I said to be polite. But I was really humoring him. Of course, I was going to start out hard. I was there to compete.

I took off over the bridge, part of a tide of humans all working toward the same goal. I made my way into Brooklyn, where I saw Orthodox rabbis along the course in Williamsburg. I cycled into Queens, where I rode in parallel to the Manhattan skyline on the other side of the East River. I kept pushing, my arms full of heat, as mile after mile went by under the autumn sun. That Bravo Company sign was blowing in the wind behind me.

Spectators lined the street a dozen deep when I rounded off the Queensboro Bridge onto First Avenue and into Manhattan. The feeling of the roadway was so electric that I could barely feel the wheels under me. The crowd was roaring encouragement. I kept pushing. The crowd was exploding with whistles and applause. My heart was pounding with excitement, and I felt like I could float up off the pavement. The wind rushed past. I felt like a real athlete again.

When I crossed the finish line in Central Park after those grueling 26.2 miles, it was so powerful and cathartic. My body had been pushed to its absolute limits, but my mind felt so strong. With my medal hanging proudly around my neck, I had proven to myself that I was still a competitor. I would still cross finish lines. I could still push through limits when every muscle was trying to tell me to stop. So what if I looked different?

Chapter 16

On the Mountaintop

I was back at Walter Reed a week later when I saw another sign-up sheet. This one was a notice for a December ski trip with the Vail Veterans Program. I wrote my name down without hesitation. I was now all in on returning to the life of an athlete, and my competitive restlessness had returned with full force.

With a little convincing, my fellow wounded vet, Dawn, signed up as well. We were each allowed to bring one other person with us, so we invited our Ward 57 nurses, Erica and Margret, as a way of saying thanks for all they had done for us. A few weeks later, the four of us set off to board a plane for Vail, Colorado.

I had been told that flying as an amputee presented some original challenges. They were right.

Beep! Beep! Beep!

I was standing in a long line of people going slowly through airport security when my prosthetic leg set off all the alarms. The TSA agents circled around me, and I felt hundreds of eyes staring at me as though I had done something wrong. Then it was time for extra pat-downs and security swabs. I felt one of those "why me?" moments coming on. I was a patriot, after all, not a terrorist trying to travel. (To this day, I often dread all the extra time it takes me to travel and get through airport security. I have to remind myself to see the big picture and that people are just trying to do their jobs and keep people safe.)

The mountains of Vail filled me with the same excitement that I had felt the first time I saw Boulder—that magic of the sun-kissed snowy heights of Colorado. At the resort, there were dozens of other wounded veterans, soldiers who had been traumatically injured and were there to either learn to ski again or learn to get down the hill for the first time.

Having all these other veterans around me was comforting. There was an immediate sense of camaraderie between all of us—there were so few other people who had gone through what we had. The town of Vail seemed to come alive for us, welcoming the wounded veterans with open arms for five days of luxurious accommodations and delicious dinners. I think, for all of us, the process of healing was ongoing, and the support we felt from all around us kept us on the right side of the road.

I had loved skiing when I was growing up—what wasn't there to love about the speed, the challenge, the rush—so it was a big deal for me to be learning it again. My parents flew out to meet me on the mountain and watch.

The first day was a battle. I hesitantly rode up the magic carpet as I did nineteen years before when I was a kid learning how to ski. I got off the lift and stood staring down from the top

One of the first trophies I ever won.

My Gym Elite days.

My sister Amanda and I on Dad's lap.

With my tough-love coach Olga Korbut.

College graduation, complete with a flag painted on top of my cap.

Amanda and I after my commissioning ceremony.

In Kuwait in full battle gear days before heading into Iraq.

My vehicle and my blood after the roadside bomb hit us.

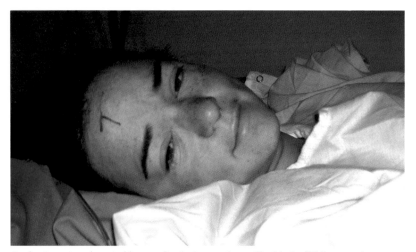

In the American hospital hours after losing my leg, still with the 'T' for tourniquet.

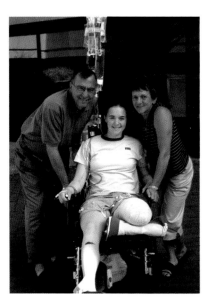

At Walter Reed with my parents, always strong and steadfast by my side.

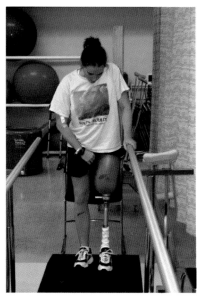

Standing up for the first time with my prosthetic leg.

Swimming made me feel whole again.

Riding through the streets of Copacabana Beach in Rio to a bronze medal finish. (Photo courtesy of Joe Kusumoto.)

Sharing the podium in Rio with my teammates, Hailey and Allysa, on Sep 11, 2016. One of the greatest moments of my life. (Photo courtesy of Joe Kusumoto.)

Sharing a dance with President George W. Bush in a picture that he painted for his book *Portraits of Courage*. (Photo by Layne Murdoch, Jr. / Courtesy George W. Bush Presidential Center.)

My husband Brian and I with our best dog Jake about to start the W100 mountain bike ride with President Bush on his ranch in Texas.

A surreal moment, standing among all the living Presidents and their spouses before the opening of the George W. Bush Presidential Library. (Photo by Paul Morse/ Courtesy George W. Bush Presidential Center)

My wedding bridesmaids and best friends, Megan, Brandi, Keri, Stephanie, Tiffany, and Amanda. (Photo by Joshua Albanese.)

Dare2tri co-founders, Dan, Keri, and myself.

Speaking to a corporate group about the power of choice.

My beautiful kids, Dallas and Millie.

My family, and my everything. (Photo courtesy of Christopher Austin @austinstudi-odenver, 2019.)

Doing my best to balance being an elite athlete and a mom. (Courtesy of Jill Dahl.)

of the bunny hill. I was nervous and skeptical, but excitement overcame both, as I knew there was nothing else I could do, but head for the bottom. It turned out there is really no guidebook for figuring out how to ski on one leg. It was all going to be trial and error, and it was all going to be up to me.

We used outrigger poles that had little skis on the end for balance. Perched on my one leg, I pushed against the ground with those poles and slowly shifted down the gentle slope. I started unintentionally drifting left and right, then back again, not under control. I felt like a lost dog in the snow, weaving this way and that. It was embarrassing. I fell hard and got a face full of snow. I felt like a little kid again, and not in the best way.

Eventually, I got the help of a personal instructor, Dave, who I'm still friends with today. He helped me come to grips with my balance, and to use my three points of contact with the snow to find a groove and use gravity to help me rather than lead me astray. I started to take the chair lift farther and farther up the mountain. I wobbled less and fell fewer times.

By the end of the fifth day, I found myself at the top of the mountain. I was with Dave, my parents, and a few others who had tagged along. But, as I paused to look down the mountain, it felt for a moment as though it was only me alone there—just me and the eerie silence. The sun shone and glared off the snow and the view stretched out for what felt like hundreds of miles.

It was a long way down. All the way down. *Can I make it?*

I wasn't going to get to the bottom by standing there thinking about it.

Go!

My ski crushed into the snow. I picked up speed. I had purpose and force. The world started to accelerate before my eyes, and the wind whistled in my ears.

Maybe I had grown up loving to ski, but that run felt like my first.

When I reached the bottom I skidded to a stop—I had to avoid all the prosthetic limbs and wheelchairs lying around. It was an incredible sight as if everyone had shed the memory of their injuries. All of the soldiers were up there on the mountain somewhere, learning to ski, feeling the motion and balance, and discovering what was possible with their new bodies.

I never felt as alive as I did that week on the ski hill. And I never felt as proud of a group of people as I did my fellow wounded veterans. I've been back to Vail nine times since, in a mentorship role for the program that brought me there. Everyone's life is made better by going past our limits, and, for amputees, it's as true as for anyone.

Chapter 17

Make the Most of a Second Chance

I had heard that good things in life come in threes. This turned out to be true for me, after completing the New York City Marathon and learning to ski again in Vail. The rule of three was proved true by a third outdoor adventure that continued to help me propel past all the obstacles that had fallen into my path.

The Wounded Warrior Project's Soldier Ride brought wounded veterans from city to city in the United States, riding bicycles or handcycles for a few hours each day through towns full of people waving American flags at us and cheering us on.

This gave me the opportunity to ride an upright bike again for the first time since my injury. It wasn't easy. At that point, I didn't own a prosthetic biking leg yet, so Little Leg hung off to one side of the bicycle seat as I pedaled with my one leg through Baltimore, Washington DC, Chicago, and Denver.

I had to think of Sweet Thunder as I felt the wind and the speed from the seat of that upright bike. It wasn't always easy to balance, especially over variable terrain. I wore an elbow pad on my left side in case of falls.

During those rides, I recognized and reconnected with other soldiers who I had seen in New York and Vail. I noticed how quickly a lot of them had progressed physically. One soldier who hadn't even been able to walk on his prosthetic leg in New York but had been able to give skiing a go in Colorado, was now walking almost perfectly by the time I saw him at Soldier Ride.

The camaraderie I shared with these other patriots as we watched one another in our respective journeys was transcendent. Nothing felt better than cheering each other on in this second chance at life. It was nice to have compatriots with whom I could share the recovery process. It was also profound to share the memory and the respect for all of those who hadn't been as fortunate as us, who hadn't made it home.

* * *

I realized that the thing that drew every phase of my life together was being an athlete. Gymnastics, swimming, pole vaulting—pretty much any sport you could name, I had given it a try at one point or another, and often in formal competition.

My priority at Walter Reed had been to simply get back on my feet again and live an independent life, the same as every other soldier there. Now that I had gotten a taste of that life *and* ways to compete as an athlete again, I wanted more.

I cultivated that unique desire. To feel the hard work every athlete puts in, the sweat, the burning muscles, the triumph over doubt, the finish lines. I had tasted it again, and I wanted to keep tasting it. I was going to pursue every opportunity to get back into sport that presented itself to me.

The jubilation of crossing the finish in New York, the freedom of skiing down the mountain in Vail under the bright sun, then going back to Walter Reed and building on the new strength I was finding in my body—I had come a long way in a short time, and overcome a lot of pain and uncertainty, and I felt like I could do anything I set my mind to. Participating in competition again was giving me so much confidence and self-worth, reminding me of what sport has to offer and teaching me new things about myself as my recovery went on.

I would never understate how difficult it is for anyone to come back from the kind of injury I experienced, whether on a wartime battlefield or in civilian life. I do know that, after my amputation, I still had the same restlessness I always had, the same determination to keep moving, the same intensity. The question was where I was going to put it.

The choice to jump back into sports after losing my leg probably saved my life. It definitely redefined my destiny.

* * *

By 2005, I was down to about two weekly visits to Walter Reed. I knew I was on schedule to be discharged entirely in a couple of months. On one of my visits, I was literally twiddling my thumbs waiting for an appointment when I saw another one of those sign-up sheets. It was a new one, which piqued my interest.

U.S. Paralympics.

I didn't know what that was—which, looking back, is pretty crazy. But I thought, *Okay, I'll go and learn about this thing, whatever it is.*

I was always going to go to whatever it was. Those sign-up sheets were keeping my heart beating.

When I arrived at the introductory session, in walked a robust guy with the kind of booming voice you can hear from across a field. *Like God*, I thought. *Or maybe Morgan Freeman.*

It was John Register, a former NCAA All-American who had become a Paralympic medalist after losing a leg in a freak hurdling accident that led to an amputation. He strolled to the front of the room to address the veterans who had shown up that day. He commanded the room from the moment he entered. As soon as he opened his mouth, I thought, *Okay, I'm going to do whatever this guy tells me to do.*

He talked in a you-can-do-anything, inspirational voice that was totally sincere and authentic. He explained what the Paralympics were: essentially the Olympics for people with disabilities, taking place two weeks after the Olympics and in the same venues.

"The competitions are *extremely competitive*," John said, and I paid even closer attention.

He explained that, for those of us who trained hard enough, this was a chance to compete on the world's biggest athletic stages. We could wear a USA uniform and represent our country—just the way I had done with pride in Iraq. I sat there, my mouth hanging open and my eyes fixated on John—I was in awe of the concept. Of course, I had dreamed of going to the Olympics as a gymnast when I was young, and here was someone telling me that there was a second chance, even after losing my leg.

It was one of those moments when time seems to stop. A second chance at the Olympics.

I thanked John after his talk. I knew then that somehow, someway, I was going to become a Paralympian. The next Paralympic Games were three years out, in Beijing in 2008.

It wasn't as though you could just sign up—not like the military. You needed to clock times beforehand in competition against the best in the world. Beating that competition was going to be a lofty goal, but I was dead set on it.

This was my new dream. This was my purpose. I had finally settled on the biggest challenge that I was going to try to meet in my new life on one leg.

* * *

First, I had to medically retire from the Army. In April of 2005, all my paperwork for discharge was done and approved. My service to my country was complete—at least, in one capacity.

My final sendoff from active military life happened a week before my last trip to Walter Reed. It was fitting because it also happened to be my first Alive Day.

I learned all about other soldiers' Alive Days at Walter Reed—the anniversary of the day a soldier lost whatever they had lost. Instead of mourning, it became their Alive Day—a celebration of making it through. From the moment I heard of this tradition, I thought it was a genius idea. I decided to take the concept one step further and name my day after my leg. From then on out, April 13 would be known as Little Leg's birthday, and, every year, I was going to throw a party for her.

Little Leg's first birthday party was one of the most meaningful days of my life. It was a lighthearted celebration. Dozens of people came to our house that night. Anyone and everyone I had met during my rehab at Walter Reed was invited—the more, the merrier. My surgeon, my physical therapist, my occupational therapist, and many of the other wounded soldiers were there, along with many of my family and friends. I spent a huge part of the evening thanking them again and again for helping me get to this point.

Everyone got a nametag when they came into the house. Mine said, *Little Leg Owner*, and anyone else who had lost a limb the year before got a nametag of their own that said, *Little Leg Class of 2004*. My physical therapist got one that read, *Little Leg's Coach*.

There was a lot of laughter. Dick and I had done a photo-shoot with Little Leg in advance of the party and enlarged a picture of her in a little red hat on a huge banner that read: *Life is Good*. We hung American flags and handed out party hats. There was a lot of food and drink and, of course, a birthday cake for Little Leg. The walls were lined with photos from my year of recovery. We had two piñatas, one in the form of a Jeep and the other a pirate with a peg leg. We took turns whacking them on our screened-in back porch, and, when it exploded, it wasn't candy that came out—it was as many of my empty medication bottles from Walter Reed as I could collect in one place.

Tammy Duckworth and I took turns hitting that Humvee, both wearing blindfolds. It was one of the few times that I had outwardly expressed anger in front of my family and friends after losing my leg. Getting it out of my system felt good. It felt good to release it now that I was embracing a new value on what the rest of my life meant. It felt like being reborn.

* * *

On April 20, 2005—one year, one week, and one leg after the IED explosion on the road to the Green Zone in Iraq—I was discharged from Walter Reed and medically retired from the

Army. It was technically a dual retirement because I was both honorably and medically discharged. I had my Purple Heart from the hospital commander, and he thanked me for my service to my country and for my sacrifice. I was also given a Bronze Star, which a soldier receives when someone nominates them for going above and beyond the call of duty.

Honestly, I didn't think that I had gone above and beyond the call of duty. I had been doing my job, and I had been in the wrong place at the wrong time. But my commander thought I should receive a Bronze Star, he nominated me, and I received it.

As the years pass, I am even more proud of those medals and the meaning behind them.

That same month, my unit returned home from its year-long tour of duty in Iraq and had a welcoming ceremony at Fort Hood. I flew down there to be with everyone I had served with and to welcome them home. It was actually a little awkward. They had all been together nonstop for the past year without me and had shared a lot of experiences that I didn't and gotten much closer as a result. It was also the first time they had seen me with one leg. There were hugs and well wishes, and a sense of closure. There was always going to be a big difference in our military experiences.

The next month, I kept moving. I wrapped up my coursework at community college and was accepted into the prosthetics program at Century College, a trade school in White Bear Lake, Minnesota. It was a little bit like going home since I'd spent high school in the Land of 10,000 Lakes and still had a lot of friends there. It felt great to finally be somewhere familiar after spending the past several years in Army bases and in the hospital.

Dick was also able to keep moving forward, signing up to attend the University of Minnesota to take the prerequisites he needed in order to get back on track and start medical school—his next big leap in life. We moved to Minnesota during the warm months of summer when the lakes glisten under the sun and we had time to get adjusted to a new home before starting school in the fall.

I Googled for swim teams in the Twin Cities area, feeling like the clock was ticking on my dream of the 2008 Paralympics. I called up a handful of coaches who had club teams, explaining myself when they picked up the phone.

"Hi, my name's Melissa. I lost my leg over in Iraq a year ago," I'd say. There was no point in a lot of preliminaries. "I want to compete as a swimmer in the Paralympic Games. Can you help get me there?"

I got momentary silence on the line from the first few coaches I called. My story didn't click with any of them until I reached Jim Anderson, coach of the competitive Twin Cities Swim Team.

"Yeah, sure," he replied. "Why don't you come on over? We'd love to have you."

He was as inviting and warm in person as he was on the telephone. It didn't take long for me to join the Twin Cities Swim Team, and to start practicing with them at the University of Minnesota pool.

It was going to be a long road to Beijing, but I had a feeling it was starting right here.

Chapter 18

Competing Against Myself

I arrived at the pool deck for my first day of practice at the facility. The place was high ceilinged and echoey, with the pool marked off into lanes and permanent spectator seating running lengthwise along either side of the water.

One thing was clear right away: I was one of the oldest swimmers there. This was a club team made up primarily of high school and college kids.

I paused after I came through the doorway, hearing the familiar splash of lap swimmers. *What am I doing here?* I had been so enthusiastic about signing up, but now I felt a wave of doubt and hesitancy.

My walking on the prosthetic was getting better every day, but I didn't wear it to come out to the pool. I scanned the tiles of the deck as I moved carefully with my crutches. The last thing I wanted to do was take a fall in front of everyone before I even knew their names. I was the only swimmer there who was missing a limb, and falling would probably make them treat me as though I was disabled.

When I managed to overcome my reservations and join the group, I was assigned the lane for the slowest swimmers. *Okay*, I thought. *I get it.* I was old, I was slow, I was the most disabled. I felt alienated from everyone there, and it wasn't a good sensation. I got into the water and tried to just focus on my stroke, moving through the water, concentrating on my form. It helped, but I still didn't feel as though I belonged.

I got through the first practice, but, even as I carefully made my way back to the locker room, I wasn't able to summon that fire for sports that had brought me there.

"Just give it a shot," Dick said when I told him how I felt.

He was a big supporter of me returning to the world of athletics. All of my family and friends were unfailingly supportive when I talked about the Paralympics. Instead of just leaving the pool that day and never going back, I tried to focus on their belief in me. I would keep at it.

Maybe it was part of my re-entry into life after the Army and the hospital, or maybe it was because of my missing leg. Maybe it was because I found it hard to interact with some of the younger swimmers, but, for whatever reason, I found myself pretty closed off during my first months with the team. I didn't talk to a lot of people. I didn't even change in the locker room. I would swim, pull myself out of the pool, and wrap my towel around me so that I could drive home by myself and change there.

I wasn't sure why I was doing this. When I gave it some thought, I had to admit that I was feeling overwhelmed. This was all so new. I was a recent amputee. I had just gotten out of the Army. I felt this restless drive inside me, but I was also having a hard time adjusting in certain situations—and the swim team seemed to bring all of that to the surface.

I was also learning to truly swim again, and it wasn't coming as easily as I would have liked. Finally, one day one of the high schoolers waved at me as I was carefully balancing on my crutches after a swim.

"Hey, Melissa," she said as she came up to me. She seemed very young. "Come on and change in the locker room with the rest of us. We never get a chance to talk."

From that day, the ice was broken, and I joined the younger women in the locker room after each practice. Before long, I was chatting and joking as though I had known them for years. That pulled me out of being so inward-focused, and I was able to relax and find that friendship among teammates that was such a wonderful aspect of athletics. I became more comfortable being the amputee swimmer.

* * *

I took it seriously. I swam with the club five days a week, and, on three of those, I swam twice a day. I had always been a good swimmer and knew all the competitive strokes from the time I was growing up, but now there were a lot of challenges to performing competitive moves with one leg: diving off the block, executing flip turns, pushing off the wall. I prepared and prepared for my first meet, feeling that anxiety that comes with the unknown quality of trying something for the first time.

At my first swim meet with the team, I dove off the blocks and hit the water. It was a decent swim, but I performed a flip turn incorrectly.

One of the officials on the pool deck immediately raised her flag, which meant that I would be disqualified. I finished my swim and pulled myself carefully out of the pool. I had a ways to go and tried not to show my frustration to my teammates.

I looked up and saw the official who had flagged me coming my way. I thought she was going to explain my disqualification, but she surprised me.

"Never mind, you're good, honey," she said. She had clearly just noticed that I was missing a leg. "Don't worry about it."

This threw me off. My times at that meet didn't really matter for any official tally, so I wasn't overly upset about the prospect of being DQ'd. But I really didn't know what to think, and I felt a mixed bag of conflicting emotions. It was one of the first times I felt that I was getting special treatment because I was an amputee. I didn't know if this was a good or bad thing. I knew I wouldn't get any special treatment if I was actually able to make it to the Paralympics.

I finished last in my first few races. My placement didn't matter because I was actually competing against myself, getting official times to qualify for the Can Am Swimming Championships—which was the next big meet for para-swimmers in the Americas. That was taking place in 2006, fortunately enough, at the same pool at the University of Minnesota. I had become 100 percent fixated on the Can Am meet, because of its location where I swim nearly every day and because of its role as a stepping stone to the Paralympics.

My times gradually got faster, but it was a slog at times. I didn't have any real support then from a Paralympic team or program, and I was pursuing this dream on my own. I relied a lot on Jim for coaching. One day, I was joined by another swimmer who gave me some inspiration as well as competition.

Anna Eames was another Minnesota swimmer who was trying to make the qualifying times for the Can Am meet. Anna was born with fibular hemimelia, a condition that caused her right fibula to be shorter than her left. It was fun and encouraging to have someone else at the pool who was working toward the same goal as me.

On the other hand, Anna grew up with her disability and had been swimming with it for her entire life. She made the Can Am qualifying times pretty quickly. I realized then that I was going to be competing with a lot of people who had been born with their disabilities and were a lot more adjusted to them than I was. It made a dramatic difference, and it was stark to realize to what degree I was playing catch-up. Not only was I learning to swim with one leg, but I was also trying to become a competitive swimmer and clock the kind of times that would gain entry to international meets—where the competition would be even stiffer. It was going to be even tougher than I had originally thought when I wrote my name on that sign-up sheet and felt like I was going to conquer the world.

Then, at one meet, I did it. My stroke was becoming more fluid, my kicks more dynamic, and I felt a better sense of strength and balance in the water. Even though I was still effectively competing against myself, at a meet, I clocked an official time that qualified me for the Can Ams.

I was elated as I pulled myself out of the pool and learned my time. It felt like a huge breakthrough, but a more sobering reality followed as I toweled myself off: My times were still far short from those posted by the national team. National team times got you noticed: Coaches would pay more attention, there would be potential funding for meets, and it was a pathway to the Paralympics.

But I still had a chance. At I sat down, I thought: *That's all I need. A chance.*

The door hadn't closed on me.

* * *

The Can Ams arrived at the end of 2006. Before I could compete, I had to be officially classified as a para-swimmer. Every para-athlete has to be classified before they can compete, and they are put into a group based on the degree of activity limitation resulting from their disability. This is intended to create a level and fair playing field as much as possible since there is a pretty wide range of disabilities.

I showed up for my classification appointment, with my required documentation in hand from my doctor with all the information about my disability, including how I got it and how my rehabilitation had gone. There were medical personnel on hand who evaluated a lot of factors: my range of motion in each limb, then how well my limbs functioned in the water. At the time, there were ten different swimming classifications, with S1 for the most disabled athletes and S10 for the least disabled.

I got classified as an S9. That gave me an official confirmation of what times I would need to hit if I was ever going to join the national team.

* * *

The Can Ams were a three-day meet with swimmers from all over Canada and America. It was the biggest competition that I'd ever been a part of and the first in which I was surrounded entirely by competitors who had disabilities. Wheelchairs were everywhere. Prosthetic legs lined the pool deck. Blind athletes' canes were stacked against the walls. There were dozens of athletes with every kind of disability, and they were all gathered at the pool where I trained and swam.

I looked around at them, simply in awe. I wanted to be like them.

I didn't know most of them at the point, but I soon got to know the names of some of the best athletes, such as Jessica Long, and Rudy Garcia-Tolson. Even as the athletes assembled and started warming up, it was clear to me that this was a welcoming community. I'd get to know a lot of the athletes, as well as a lot of the coaches in those three days.

I didn't make the national standards at the Can Am meet, but I knew that I probably shouldn't have expected to. I soaked up the friendship, watched the other athletes compete and, maybe most importantly, I hit my goal of improving my times.

My times were getting better and better.

Chapter 19

It Is What It Is

I knew that I wasn't going to quit. I kept at it, training at the pool twice a day. I could feel myself getting stronger, cutting through the water with more certainty.

There was still a ways to go for me to hit the cutoff times for the national team. Over the coming months, I traveled to more para-swimming meets in the United States, as well as a couple in Canada. I dug into my well of determination to keep improving my times. I hoped that I was making a name for myself, that I was being perceived as a contender for the national swim team. But I knew that I wasn't on anyone's radar in a major way—no one was, not until they actually qualify for the team.

I swung between devotion and doubt. No matter how hard I worked, it looked like I was a total longshot for making the next Paralympics. It wasn't an easy thing to make the team in such a short time. I had to face the fact that my times might be improving, but that they weren't close to where they needed to be.

Still, I wasn't going to quit.

The U.S. Paralympic trials were going to be in April of 2008—I had the date circled on my calendar. It took on the quality of a be-all, end-all moment looming in the near future. It was more than a goal. It was something that was making me feel normal again.

* * *

I didn't just swim, of course. I was balancing life as a full-time student, studying prosthetics at Century College, and being a wife. My first year was in the technician program, where I learned how to fabricate a leg socket—a big breakthrough for me.

Never in the past had I been a handy person or worked with any kind of large tools. If anything needed to be fixed, I relied on someone else to do it. Now, at school, I was learning my way around heavy equipment, and dealing with carbon fiber, fiberglass, and laminations to mold limbs and create prosthetic sockets. I started to feel that I was coming full circle in a way, learning to change lives the way mine had been unlocked when I got my first prosthesis.

Without realizing it all at once, I was morphing into a handy person. Anyone who knew me when I was younger was pretty amazed. I learned how to use a bandsaw, a heat gun, Allen wrenches, and all kinds of special screwdrivers. I loved learning about all of it, soaking up information and even starting to become handier around the house—all it takes is a little skill and some problem-solving.

The second year in school was made up of the practitioner program, where I learned more about anatomy and different phases of the dynamic system called the gait pattern—then how it all related to prosthetics. People who were missing a limb would come to our classes and let us practice on them by making custom sockets for them to try. For some classes, I served as a model, letting other students learn by practicing on my leg.

I came to realize that I wanted to be a practitioner rather than a technician. I loved working directly with patients, rather than spending all my time in the backroom fabricating prosthetics. I wanted to show others how their lives didn't have to end or be severely limited when they lost a leg or other limb.

I wanted to be able to say, and show: *Look at me. I did it, and so will you.*

This was the beginning of a feeling that I had something to share with the world that was much larger than myself.

I graduated from Century College in May of 2007. I was asked to give the commencement address to thousands of people—my first public speech, with many more to come.

Like a lot of inexperienced speakers, I kind of had an out-of-body experience. I don't remember exactly what I said. I'm willing to bet it was cheesy. I remember I brought a lot of song lyrics into my speech, along with inspirational quotes. I might have been rough around the edges, but my message was well-received: I got my first-ever standing ovation from the crowd.

* * *

While I was wrapping up prosthetics school, Dick was completing all his requirements to apply to medical school. He got accepted into Loyola University's medical school in Chicago, and we would move there together.

I needed to do a year-long residency in prosthetics before I could take the board certification exam, so I applied for and was accepted to be a resident at Scheck and Siress Prosthetics, also in Chicago. I was working under residency director Dave Rotter, a certified prosthetist and orthotist, and one of the best in the business. That's no exaggeration—people fly in from all over the country to work with him—and we became fast friends. I started to rotate to work with different experts in the lab to optimize my experience for the board exams. I also started receiving care at Scheck & Siress, with Dave becoming my personal prosthetist. That part of life felt as though it was really coming together in the shape of a future.

With all that, my dream of being a Paralympian wasn't going anywhere—I was able to transfer it to Chicago. I joined up with the local Northwestern Wildcats Club swim team, and, this time, I had enough confidence not to keep to myself and leave dripping wet with a towel around my head after practice.

I threw myself into it the same way I had in Minnesota. I started leaving the house at five in the morning to train before work, then I'd head back to the pool when my day at Scheck & Siress was done. My days were longer and busier than at any time since I returned from Iraq.

I loved it. I remembered those quiet afternoons when I was an outpatient at Walter Reed, wondering what I was going to find to feed my hunger for staying active and occupied.

The Paralympics dream stayed at the front of my mind. Three months into my prosthetics training, I got an email about an athlete residency program for wounded veterans at the U.S. Olympic Training Center in Colorado Springs. I read it carefully.

Athletes interested in trying to make the Paralympic team could go live there in the athlete dorms, train full time, with all their expenses completely covered. There was access to some of the best training facilities and equipment in the world.

I was conflicted about the opportunity. I felt torn about whether or not I should go after this. I really wanted to take advantage of this chance, but I didn't want to leave Dick alone in Chicago dealing with the difficult challenge of medical school. He had stuck by my side and given me so much strength through everything that I had been through. I wondered if it would be selfish of me to go a thousand miles away, even if it offered a real road toward my dream.

* * *

I think today that that was the beginning of the end of my relationship with Dick. I knew he wanted to be supportive of me, but he had reservations about us living apart.

Maybe it was selfish of me, but I ended up choosing to leave everything behind in Chicago, including Dick, to pursue my Paralympic dream. It probably wasn't the best move for our relationship, and I probably knew that at the time. But it was also the kind of opportunity that was so difficult to pass up, especially after so much time trying to get coaching on club teams and putting in countless hours essentially racing against myself. Scheck & Siress granted me permission to put my residency on hold while I tried to make the Paralympic team, with a promise to hold my spot for me until I returned. Everything back home would have to stay on hold for the time being, I thought.

Dick and I drove out together from Chicago to the U.S. Olympic Training Center in Colorado Springs. Dick stayed with me the first few nights, then he flew back to Chicago. He helped me set up my new dorm room, complete with a hot water heater, so my sweet tooth could have some hot chocolate at the end of the day. As hard as it was to say goodbye to him, I was also invigorated to be back in the mountains of Colorado. I was in a beautiful little city nestled at the eastern foot of the Rocky Mountains; it was an easy trade-off, to switch the Chicago skyscrapers and busy freeways with the red sandstone and snow-capped mountain views.

The Olympic Training Center turned out to be like a mini college campus. It had a central dining hall flanked by athletes' dorms, which were in turn at the edge of two lines of gyms that houses state-of-the-art training facilities. There was a fifty-meter swimming pool, a wrestling center, a facility for shooting, and gyms devoted to gymnastics, basketball, wheelchair rugby, and goalball. People from all over the world came there not only to train for tours but to take in historical photos and inspirational quotes from past Olympians and Paralympians.

There was an air of excellence about the place that I was eager to breathe in every day. Athletes came there for a single goal: to become the best, to elevate their performance to world-class.

I felt like a college student again when I moved into the dorms. I was among dozens of other Olympic and Paralympic hopefuls training in their respective sports—my target was the 2008 games in Beijing, but, deep inside, I didn't really think of myself as a candidate for the games at the time. In fact, I was far from it. I had yet to make national team times and was considered an outside candidate for making it. I was allowed to be there because of my wounded veteran status, but I was resolved to make the most of it.

The first time I walked into the Olympic Training Center pool, I was completely awestruck. It was like no other pool I'd ever trained in, lined with the colorful flags from all the Olympics and Paralympics host cities. It felt historic, and the atmosphere in there was serious and businesslike.

I was one of seven on the resident Paralympic swim team. By then, I was twenty-eight, which made me the oldest athlete on our team by nearly a decade. I had a college degree and was on track for a professional career. I was a war veteran. Most of my teammates weren't old enough to drink. Pretty quickly, I fell into an older-sister role with them.

I met our coach, Jimi Flowers. I could tell right away that he was an incredible person, and one of the most kind-hearted individuals I'd ever met—he would soon have an enormous impact on my life. Jimi frequently wore a tie-dyed T-shirt and was typically holding a coffee mug decorated with a peace sign. He was a laid-back guy, especially for a sports coach, and wore a smile all day long. We all thought of him as a walking exclamation point, an ambassador of positivity. His job was to be dedicated to the seven of us.

It is what it is, he would say.

That was a phrase that would stay with me in the years to come whenever challenges presented themselves. Jimi was the kind of person who left an impression on everyone he met, even if it was just for a few seconds.

In addition to a dedicated coach, we also had access to some of the best nutritionists, sports psychologists, and physical therapists in the country while we were staying there. The resources on that campus were incomparable, and it was only in that environment that I stood a chance of elevating my performance to a national- or world-class level.

Of course, nothing came easy.

Chapter 20

Finding Something Greater than Myself

I hit the water first thing in the morning, serenaded by Kanye West's "Good Morning" blasting from the pool's speakers in the pre-dawn hour. Jimi had written today's inspirational quote on the whiteboard we all saw before we started practice. My body was sore all over.

This was even harder than I thought it was going to be, and I knew it was going to be hard.

Back in Chicago, I would swim, go to work, have a second swim some days, and then have a social life. At the Olympic Training Center, it was different. I swam. I ate. I swam. I ate. I slept. Then I did it all again the next day. I got up at seven in the morning to start training and went to bed at nine at night after two to three practices a day. I was swimming more hours a day than I ever had—sometimes more than 10,000 meters in a day. My shoulders burned. My entire body was exhausted.

My entire focus in life became one simple thing: swim faster.

I loved it. I knew I was doing the right thing.

Jimi called out encouragement. Sometimes it felt like he believed in us more than we believed in ourselves.

When I started, I couldn't keep up with my teammates. As the weeks passed, I gradually got closer to them in the pool.

Everything was on another level. I was training in the same pool as some of the best athletes in the world. Swimming groups would come through the facility regularly, including famous names. I got used to the reality of swimming multiple times in the same pool as Olympic legend Michael Phelps—I'd run into him on the pool deck, but I was always too nervous to approach him and ask for a picture. All of us on the team were equally star-struck at moments such as that one.

Throughout the spring, I competed in local competitions in Colorado Springs, as well as a few others throughout the country. Even though I was improving, I was on a pretty tight timeline if I wanted to make the Paralympics that September. I'd been training hard for two years by then. My times were a lot better, but it felt as though my progress was slowing down.

A camera started following me around Colorado Springs for a documentary project called *Warrior Champions* documenting the journey of a few athletes from Baghdad to Beijing. In my case, getting to China felt far from given. The crew filmed me at a meet at the U.S. Air Force Academy, where my performance was horrible, and my times were nothing close to where they needed to be. The crew drove back with me to the Olympic Training Center after that meet, and I was so upset that I couldn't maintain my composure while they were filming.

"If I'm going to swim like that," I said, burning with anger at myself. "Then this is never going to happen."

* * *

When I wasn't at the pool, there really wasn't much else to do. The Olympic Training Center, for all of the people living and working there, can be a lonely place. You train and you train (and train some more), but, unless you have others around of a similar age and mindset, you're kind of on your own when you're not working. I loved my teammates—we spent hours upon hours together, and we encouraged each other and built each other up—but there was no denying the age gap between us. Between training sessions in the pool, my teammates would go to classes at the local community college or go back to their rooms to play video games until we were called back to the pool.

We would hang out after dinner for a few hours, and, more than once, I found myself playing Rock Band with my teammates. I'd belt out whatever song was chosen on the microphone as the lead singer.

More often, I'd end up by myself at Starbucks, passing the time with a book to keep me company. I got caught up reading *Boys in the Boat, Touch the Top of the World*—any sort of story of strength and overcome challenges. I had a keyboard my sister had laying around and gave me to pass the time, and I started taking lessons (my shining moment was learning to play "Puff the Magic Dragon"). I'd do anything to keep busy, to keep moving forward, to banish that downtime and keep the momentum going.

* * *

Almost four years to the day after I lost my leg to that road-side bomb, I walked onto the pool deck at the University of

Minnesota to race in the U.S. Paralympic Trials. It was the same pool where I'd trained with the Twin Cities Swim Team, and the site of my first major competition at the Can Ams.

I walked into that particular chlorine smell, the spectator stands, the unique way that room sounded when it was full of people. My eyes landed on the lane where this had all started, when I was relearning to swim and when I was the slowest swimmer on the club team. It was like coming home.

Anyone would have considered me a longshot that day to make the Paralympic team. I still hadn't qualified for the national team. My times just weren't there. I was still fifteen seconds off in the 400-meter freestyle, and at least five seconds off in each of the other competitive events. In order to qualify for the United States Paralympic team, my time in an event would have to rank me in the top three in the world.

I had come a long way, maybe even further than I had a right to imagine. But I had never even hit a world top-20 in any event. The 400-meter freestyle was going to be my best chance to make the team, but it was a slim chance at best.

On the first day of trials, I built on and improved my best times in the hundred-meter freestyle and the hundred-meter butterfly. But it still wasn't going to be enough to make the team. When it came time for the 400-meter freestyle the next day, Jimi took me aside.

"Melissa, you got this," he told me, channeling his ocean of positivity into encouragement. "You put in the hours. This is your race."

As usual, it felt like Jimi believed in me more than I believed in myself. He gave me a hug and I made my way over to the blocks to get ready for the race.

Many of my friends and family had come to root for me; they were decked out in matching T-shirts that proclaimed them "Team Melissa." I could feel them going crazy in the stands as I narrowed my focus onto the race. I got set next to my teammate Elizabeth Stone, who was also missing a leg. She was a lot younger than me and she always beat me in everything. We exchanged glances. She was the one I needed to beat this time.

The horn went off. The swimmers hit the water. I sprinted out past Elizabeth, working hard, probably racing the first 100 meters a little more recklessly and at a faster pace than would have been prudent. I knew this was a pace that I couldn't keep up, but this was probably my last shot at the Paralympics in Beijing.

After that first 100 meters, I was way ahead. I executed my flip turn at the wall and took my breath to start the next 100. I could feel time slow down, each moment stretched as my eyes caught Jimi going crazy at the side of the pool. He was swinging his arms like a windmill. I could hear him screaming, *Go! Go! Go!*

The sound of his voice seemed to fill me with power. I pushed hard through the next 100 meters. At 200, I did an efficient flip turn and scanned the next lane. I executed my stroke, one after another after another. I was still ahead of Elizabeth by a few strokes. Jimi was going absolutely nuts, jumping up and down, his arms flailing like a wild man.

At 300 meters, I was still ahead of Elizabeth. Everything stood out stark and vivid. The wheels in my head processed the fact of what was happening as I went down into the water for my final turn. *Am I having a really good race, or is Elizabeth having a really bad one?*

I resurfaced from my turn and took a lungful of breath. Everyone I knew in the stands was on their feet and totally out of control. Jimi's energy pushed me. The energy from my loved ones pushed me. And then I began to *really* push myself, finding a reserve of energy that felt like I had never tapped it before. I sprinted those final 100 meters at a pace I didn't know I was capable of; I was surging with every muscle, pushing so hard that it felt like I was in some new world.

When I reached the finish, I hit the wall to an eruption of cheers that made the pool sound like someone had just won the Super Bowl. I was trying to catch my breath when I turned around and looked up at the scoreboard.

There was my name: Melissa Stockwell. I was listed in first place. The time next to it read: 5:03 AR.

I did a double-take. That number next to my name: was that real? Did someone make a mistake? Was this happening?

Had I really set an American record time?

As I pulled myself out of the pool, dripping with water, Jimi came running over and wrapped me in one of his signature bear hugs.

"Did I really just set a record?" I asked, my voice high, almost laughing with elation and a sense that it was impossible.

My previous times had been so far off a record, that I didn't even *know* what the American record was. I thought there was a typo, or maybe the scoreboard was broken.

I had just dropped a full twenty seconds off my morning preliminary heat. I beat Elizabeth Stone, a great swimmer. And, most importantly, my winning time put me in third place in the world. During those five minutes and three seconds, I went from being a total obscurity and a longshot to someone who had a legitimate chance.

I swam other events during the remainder of the Trials, and I was solid but didn't set any more records. My mind was fully ahead to Sunday when the team would be announced that was going to Beijing. I now thought I had a shot.

At ten in the morning on Sunday, all of the swimmers gathered in a glassed-in conference room that overlooked the pool. This is where the announcement was going to be made. The swimmers who knew they were a lock for the team were relaxed, chatty, and excited. Others like me, were sitting in anxious silence. My parents were there. I sat with Dick, the two of us making small talk to pass the time.

They started calling out the team members in alphabetical order. One by one, those called got up from their seats and walked to the front of the room. There they were handed a red-white-and-blue hockey-style jersey with the number "08" on the front and their last name stitched on the back—the jerseys reminded me of the Miracle on Ice. The team members were exchanging high-fives and hugging with happiness as the announcer reached the second half of the alphabet. I felt a rush of emotion and had to take a deep breath to try to calm myself.

"Melissa Stockwell," the voice called out.

I turned into an emotional wreck right there on the spot, before I could even get up and go to the front to claim my jersey. My eyes filled with tears. My parents and Dick were crying as well, as we all exchanged tight, emotional hugs.

Somehow, I made it up to the front, where I accepted my jersey and stood with my United States Paralympic teammates. I wiped away the tears that just kept coming.

This was a reality. I was going to be a Paralympian, swimming for Team USA at the Beijing games.

The journey from Baghdad to Beijing felt like it made sense, like a perfect circle that had closed. My choice to serve my country, my choice to stay positive through my rehab, my choice to train at the Olympic facility and work harder than I had ever imagined I could—it had all led to this turning point in my life. I felt a sense of power and purpose, and that all the decisions I had made had led me again to something greater than myself.

* * *

My plan for after the trials had been to return to Chicago— because, deep down, I hadn't really expected that I would make the team. But now I was going to Beijing in September, a fact that turned everything upside down. I decided to stay at the Olympic Training Center in the lead-up to the Paralympics, so I could continue training with Jimi and the resident team. Dick was still in the midst of medical school, but he volunteered for the summer as a medic at a Boy Scout camp outside Colorado Springs so that we could see each other more often. On Wednesdays and on the weekends, I was able to drive up to see him.

The routine was as intense as ever. But now, whenever I met someone, I no longer said, "I hope to be able to compete in the Paralympics." Instead, I said, "I'm a Paralympian."

I even said it to myself, over and over again, and it never got old.

The Paralympics take place two weeks after the Olympics, which I got to watch on TV in Colorado. I watched Michael Phelps win eight gold medals in the Water Cube, the same venue I would be swimming in. I remembered watching him train, and it was unbelievable that I would soon be competing in the same pool as an American Olympic legend.

Just a few days later, I boarded a United flight along with the rest of Team USA for Okinawa, Japan. We trained there for a week to acclimatize to the time change, getting our bodies and minds in the best condition possible before we would fly to Beijing. The long flights brought back memories of heading to Iraq just four years earlier. Only, this time, I wouldn't be wearing a military uniform to defend our country on the battle-field. I would be wearing a different uniform and representing my country on the world stage.

Chapter 21

Beijing 2008

I felt blown away the moment I stepped off the plane. We'd flown to Beijing on a charter from Japan, all of us teammates decked out in Team USA gear. Some of us were a little curious as to how we'd be received—we'd heard rumors from past games that the Paralympics athletes weren't always treated as well as the Olympic athletes, and that past organizers hadn't wanted to spend the time and money to change the signs and advertisements in the host city to reflect the games.

From the first moment we arrived in Beijing, we saw that wasn't going to be true. We were treated like royalty, as though we were indeed the finest athletes in the world.

There was a welcoming committee waiting for us at the airport, followed by a comfortable charter bus ride that took us to the Olympic Village. The city was so vibrant, so dense and bustling, with a high-tech feel and skyscrapers that went on and on. The village itself was absolutely incredible.

There were the most beautiful flowers arranged everywhere, with bridges constructed above flowing streams—like a natural wonderland that had been manufactured for the athletes. It was like a little oasis in the middle of a huge, teeming city. I was given my credentials and a badge as we signed in, and my luggage was brought to the Team USA building where I would spend the next two weeks with my teammates.

The first couple of days getting acclimated before the Opening Ceremony were surreal—especially my first look at the Water Cube. It was officially called the Beijing National Aquatics Center, but there was a good reason why the name Water Cube had stuck. It was amazing, with a honeycomb design on the outside and the inner roof; at night, it lit up with all sorts of different colors, from gorgeous purples and blues to multi-color designs. Inside, it was luxurious, with aqua-blue seating running along both sides of the beautiful pool and bright light from above that made it feel like a kind of spaceship.

My teammates and I just stood there, awestruck. Jimi was there next to me.

"I think you're a contender," he told me. "I think you might end up on the podium."

I couldn't stop swimming when I took my first warmup swim. It was such an honor to be there, representing my country along with the best of the best. I was going to give it everything I had.

* * *

The Opening Ceremony took place a few days after we arrived, the night before my first race. Some athletes opted not to walk in the ceremony if they happened to have a race the next day—they didn't want to get tired and lose their competitive edge. But this was my first Paralympics, and I didn't want to miss out on a thing.

The U.S. delegation took a group of buses to the ceremony, where we had to wait a few hours to get into the stadium—I was enjoying myself so much that I barely cared. The stadium itself was a marvel. Like the Water Cube, the Bird's Nest (as everyone called it) was built just for the 2008 games. It had a striking design, lopsided with metal bands running along its exterior that earned its nickname. Like the Water Cube, it was also amazing at night, lit up in reds and golds and reflecting its own image on the ground outside like a futuristic dream.

We walked around the outside of the stadium, where the track and field events would be held. The atmosphere was like a celebration, and I introduced myself to dozens of athletes from other countries; we also had national pins that we exchanged with each other as souvenirs. Then we were lined up by country, in alphabetical order, and started proceeding closer and closer to the stadium entrance.

Finally, we came through the main tunnel into the open air of the stadium, which was absolutely stunning. More than a dozen family and friends had come to China to cheer me on. The moment we walked onto the field, everyone around us erupted. We proudly strode out behind an American flag to a loud chant: *USA! USA! USA!*

We walked through the same kind of tunnel that NFL players emerge from, and the chant echoed off the cement walls and through the stadium as our team walked under a hail of cheers. I could see my family in the America section, easy to spot with all their American flags, and walked proudly among these athletes from all around the world—with music, and lights, the Opening Ceremony was every bit as lavish and unique as the one I had seen for the Olympians on TV a few weeks before. The organizers in Beijing spared nothing to make the event feel momentous, breathtaking, and so memorable that I had an energized and electrified feeling that I wanted to bring with me into the Water Cube. I was imagining big things. I knew that I was going to compete as hard and as well as I could possibly imagine. I went to sleep that night in the Olympic Village with those *USA* chants echoing in my ears.

* * *

I would be competing in three events in the Beijing Paralympics: the 100-meter butterfly, the 100-meter freestyle, and the 400-meter freestyle. The 400 was the race that I was really there for, the one I had the best chance of earning a medal in. I had clocked qualifying times in the other two and was happy to even have a shot at medaling in them.

The first day of competition, I had my 100-meter butterfly heat. My goal was to do the best I possibly could every morning in preliminaries because I needed to crack the top eight to qualify for the finals.

There was a separate pool where I warmed up before each race, trying to generate some heat and loosen my muscles, then I would sit with my competitors in the ready room for half an hour before heading out to the pool deck.

Some swimmers wore headphones. Others slipped glances from side to side, scouting out the competition. You could feel the nervousness in the room, and, that first day, we seemed to be waiting in there forever. I refused to put on headphones and concentrated instead on visualizing the race moment by moment while taking calming deep breaths.

It was time. The swimmers walked out to the blocks one by one as our names were announced. I made my way out onto the pool deck using my crutches. I could hear my family and friends in the stands going crazy, and I glanced up. They were waving a huge American flag and a big banner that said: *Little Leg Fan Club*. I felt a warmth inside. I wanted to do extra well just for them—it had taken time and money for each of them to come to Beijing.

I did some last-minute stretches and breathed deeply. I stepped into my start position, balanced on one leg and waited for the horn to sound.

When it did, I jumped in and swam hard two lengths of the pool. My 100-meter butterfly heat turned out pretty much like I expected: I didn't make the finals and didn't even clock a personal best. I hadn't really expected to; what was important was that I burned off some nervousness by swimming my weakest event first.

It hadn't been a bad race, and I felt pride in how hard I'd competed. I made my way through a media line of TV crews and reporters. It sunk in that I had just completed my first Paralympic race, and that gave me a high. A reporter asked me what I thought of my race.

"Well, I didn't make finals," I said, hearing confidence in my voice. "But I still have two more events to go. I'll do better."

* * *

I had to wait two days to return to the pool deck for my 100-meter freestyle heat. It almost mirrored my performance in the 100-meter fly. My fan section was dressed that day in

T-shirts that read, *Go Melissa Go,* and they brought back the flag and Little Leg banner. But, once again, I didn't make finals and didn't clock a personal best.

I had kept my expectations low for the 100, but my performance bothered me a little bit more this time around. I felt bummed as I moved through the line of reporters, but I tried not to show it as I confidently said that I still had my best event coming up.

Another two days went by. Then I was back on the pool deck for my 400-meter freestyle heat. I had woken up that morning feeling like this way my day, and everyone around me seemed to agree. Jimi gave me a pep talk that morning, telling me that I could do it—his belief was like light shining, not just on me, but on every swimmer on our team.

I soaked up Jimi's encouragement. I needed it. This race was why I was there, after setting the American record. This was my last event at the games, and it was, by far, my best event. This was going to be the race of my life.

The thirty minutes in the ready room was a sea of nerves.

I walked out to the blocks. The number 5:03—my personal best—kept running through my mind. I knew, if I could match that time, then I would qualify for the final heat. The horn went off. I dove in.

I swam 100 meters...200 meters....

Every time I got to the wall of the pool to execute my turn, I saw all of my other competitors swimming farther and farther ahead of me.

I willed my arms to move faster, pump harder, but it was like they wouldn't listen. I hit the final 100 meters and pushed. I knew that I would need to be in the top four in this heat to qualify for the final.

When I hit the finish, I looked up for my name on the board and my heart immediately sank. I wasn't going to be swimming in the finals. I had finished sixth in the heat, nowhere close to my personal best time.

My Paralympics were over, just like that.

Getting out of the pool, I was overwhelmed by a feeling of devastation. Now I had to go through that stupid media line, which was the last thing in the world that I wanted to do at that moment. I looked up at my family and friends in the stands, and I knew I wasn't able to hide my feelings. They cheered me, yelling down from above that they were proud of me and that I was a true Paralympian. I blocked out their words.

I tried to hold myself together as best I could as I made my way through the row of reporters. I told them that I had given it my best shot and that I had tried to represent my country as best I could. As I approached the end of the media line, I saw Jimi standing there, waiting for me.

I lost it. The tears started to flow. Jimi had spent the past nine months training me, and now I felt like I had completely let him down. He had believed in me. My family and my friends had believed in me. My country and my teammates had believed in me.

I had let everybody down.

It was a horrible moment, and I knew that I should have performed better. Jimi gave me a big bear hug, with just as much emotion as the day when I set an American record.

"You should be proud of yourself," he told me. "It doesn't matter how you raced today. You're a true Paralympian."

The worst part was the confusion. As Jimi tried to raise my spirits, I replayed the race in my head. Throughout my career as an athlete, it seemed that there were always good days, and there were always bad days. I hadn't felt any different that day than when I had set the record in the 400-meter freestyle. I didn't understand why. It seemed that it should have been different, after traveling all the way to China and putting everything on the line to represent my country, but it wasn't. I simply had a bad race.

"It is what it is," Jimi told me.

At that point, I needed to see my family. The only time during the Paralympics that athletes were able to see their families was when they were in the stands because competitors weren't allowed to leave the Olympic Village. But now I was done. I hadn't even cooled down yet when I called my dad, sobbing, asking if I could see everyone.

I met them upstairs in a hallway in the Water Cube, still wearing my bathing suit and walking with crutches. I hugged and cried with them, taking in their reassurances that I didn't need to earn a medal for them to be proud of me. That helped ease the pain.

* * *

All that night and the next day in the Olympic Village, I just allowed myself to be upset. I gave myself permission, I let myself feel okay about being so disappointed.

It had been a dream, but my dream didn't go the way I wanted.

The sun came up the next day. I told myself that I needed to snap out of it. My teammates were still competing, and I could help by cheering them on. I was still part of Team USA, and I was going to be a good teammate—there was no reason why my performance should have a part in ruining theirs.

Since my events were done, I was able to sit with my friends and family in the stands to watch my teammates competing. I cheered them on and stood as the anthem played when they were on the winners' podium. Of course, I wished I had been standing there like them.

The next day, there was something waiting for me on my bed in the Olympic Village dorm—it was a certificate of participation, with a little participation medal.

Are you kidding me?

I came all the way to the Beijing Paralympic Games and all I got was a lousy participation medal and certificate. I wanted to throw it out the window and leave it there. But I put it in my suitcase instead, knowing that, at some point, I would feel differently.

As the Paralympics reached the end, people kept coming up and congratulating me. *For what?* I thought. *I didn't make the podium, let alone the finals in any of my events. I didn't do well at all, why pretend otherwise?*

But, as the days went on, I realized something. They weren't telling me I had done a good job because of any of my performances in the pool—they were congratulating me for getting there. I had become a Paralympian in four years; that's what they were talking about. I had lost a leg and come back to compete on the world's biggest sporting stage in just four years.

Wandering around the village the day before the closing ceremony, I saw the two U.S. Paralympic swim team captains approaching me.

"Guess what?" they said. "You're going to be carrying the flag tomorrow."

I was taken aback. That honor was usually reserved for an athlete who had won something more than the participation medal. There were so many amazing athletes there in Beijing who had done so well for Team USA, and everyone had an amazing story, but the swim team had nominated me, and the entire Paralympic delegation had voted to confirm my selection.

That's when it truly set in for me: These Paralympics had been a lot more about the journey of getting there than it had been about my times in the pool. My journey from Baghdad to Beijing meant a lot more than any medals that I could have won.

Maybe that participation medal meant something after all.

* * *

This was a moment that triggered a new outlook on life for me. Everyone wants to be on top and dreams about being recognized as the best at something. But, so often in life, it isn't about the accolades, and the medals aren't the only meaningful reward.

What's important is overcoming the unexpected obstacles that get in your way, that derail your plans for the way you thought things were going to be. It's about having the heart to persevere. For me, this meant that I was still in the Paralympics. I got to swim in front of the world and represent my country for the second time—this time in a new uniform, but with the same pride. I got to finish the job.

* * *

All of the flag bearers from all the different countries got on an early bus bound for the Bird's Nest for the closing ceremony so that we could get fit for our flag holsters. When the time came, I walked out into the sold-out stadium for the second time, proudly holding the flag, and passionate to represent the American delegation and everything all the athletes had achieved.

I didn't stop smiling for a second.

Flashbulbs were going off everywhere. I tried to take a picture with my mind: all the flags, all the proud athletes, the stands filled with cheering people. It was a moment I want to relive again and again.

Two weeks after we returned stateside, Team USA reunited in Washington. All of the U.S. Olympians and Paralympians were brought to the White House to meet President George W. Bush and First Lady Laura Bush, and to be recognized for what everyone had accomplished in Beijing. There was an official ceremony, and then I got to experience another unforgettable moment.

The President concluded his speech praising us, and I stood next to him and presented him with the American flag that had flown over the Olympic Village in Beijing. He warmly thanked me with a presidential kiss on the cheek. I was truly starting to allow myself to feel proud of what I had done.

Every moment since I got out of the pool for the last time in Beijing has made me realize that the Paralympics are about more than individual performance. For me, it was about the journey to get into that pool, overcoming the loss of my leg, not giving in, making the hard choices that had turned a dream into reality.

Not anyone could have done what I did, and I could feel good about that. I could have chosen to dwell on my disappointing performance for months, or years, but I didn't.

Yes, I always wish I could have done better in Beijing. But I didn't, and that's okay. There were other plans in store for me. I had to choose to accept things and move on, just like I had in the days after I lost my leg.

My mindset changed as my Paralympic journey to Beijing came to an end. As soon as I got home from the White House, I found that participation medal and hung it in a place of honor. Even today, when things aren't going my way, or I'm having an off day, I look at that medal and remind myself how far I've come.

Chapter 22

Picking Up the Pieces

Returning to daily life after competing at the Paralympic Games was like coming back to reality after being involved in a big wedding. There had been so much planning and so many expectations. Now it was all over and done. *What now? What's next?*

I moved back to Chicago and back home with Dick and resumed my residency at Scheck & Siress, thankful that Dave had kept his word and saved my spot for me. I had a full year left in my residency before I could take the board exams and try to become a full-time prosthetist. The swimming pool still called out to me, but I decided to put off competitive athletics—at least, for the time being. I was thinking that I was getting pretty old by that point, and probably had nowhere to go but down in terms of being more competitive than I had been in Beijing.

A stroke of luck came my way when I was contacted by America's VetDogs, an organization that provides service dogs to wounded veterans. The call was straightforward: they asked me if I would like to participate and get my own dog.

"No, thanks," I replied immediately. "I'm so independent, I don't need a service dog. You guys should place your dogs with veterans who really need them."

Then something happened over the next couple of months. When I was out in the world, I started to notice how many other wounded soldiers had canine companions with them, and how they looked so cohesive together—I could literally feel the companionship between them. So I started to change my mind.

By December, I flew out to New York for a ten-day training session with a black lab named Jake. We worked together like it was basic training, getting to know each other and teaching him to respond to my particular voice and commands—I had lucked out because Jake had already gone through full training already. We bonded quickly, and, at the end of the training period, Jake flew back to Chicago with me. Just like that, I was a dog owner.

I had no idea how much companionship a dog provides until I got Jake. He instantly became a major part of my life. I felt like I had cheated the system because this two-year-old lab came fully trained and ready to go. If I took off my leg at home, he would bring me my crutches. If I needed something on the floor, he would pick it up for me. If I needed to walk up a set of stairs that didn't have handrails, Jake would brace his body so that I could use him for balance and leverage. He also had an athletic nature, wanting to run all the time.

Jake was a gentle and yielding service dog who showed unconditional love and devotion. He would become my best friend for the next ten years.

* * *

Jake started coming to the Scheck & Siress office with me and became our unofficial lab dog—no pun intended. I was still working under Dave and his office was situated in the basement of a hospital, in a dungeon-like atmosphere with no windows. I'd walk through the hospital and then head down through a set of hallways to the basement to an office filled with a bunch of desks. Next to the office was a lab with workbenches holding every kind of tool you could possibly think of.

On the other side of the lab was a sound-proof room with an oven for heating plastic, along with a huge exhaust system, so the workers weren't breathing chemicals all day. On the far side of the basement were all the patients' rooms. Jake loved it—he would sprint up and down the halls wagging his tail, bringing a smile to the patients. He'd do these daily strolls on his own, taking time to steal tennis balls from the physical therapy department or stuffing his face whenever he lucked out and someone brought in some peanut butter for him.

It wasn't great working in a basement, but the people I worked with made the job amazing. I loved going to work every day because of them—and I also loved the patients. I felt fortunate to have my job. In addition to being a boss, Dave also became a close friend. Dave had become renowned for creating high-end prosthetics such as running legs and legs that adapted to fit bicycles. Patients were arriving from all over the country to see him.

Some of my favorite patients were the ones who arrived in wheelchairs thinking that they would never be able to walk again. Because I wore pants to work, most of them didn't realize that I was missing a leg, even though I think I have a noticeable limp. I'd try to encourage them to take their first steps, but sometimes they would complain that it was too difficult or that it was physically impossible. When that happened, I'd pull up my pant leg and show them my prosthetic. Usually, their tense, fearful expression turned into a beam of hope at that moment. It was an incredible way of motivating them.

I loved playing my part in motivating them to stand up and walk. The joy of seeing someone realize they would walk again and regain their independence—not to mention seeing them take their first steps—was the highlight of any day. They would reclaim that power of choice and reclaim something they thought was lost. That inspired me to come to the office day after day, and, since I'd passed my board exams, I was now a certified, full-time prosthetist.

My work at Scheck & Siress had become my main focus by then, but I was still able to help coach a few swim clinics here and there, including a camp with the Challenged Athletes Foundation in San Diego. CAF is a nonprofit that provides a range of opportunities for people with disabilities, and they appreciated having a Paralympian come out and inspire the next generation of athletes with disabilities. They have an extensive grant program, and athletes can apply for financial help with adaptive equipment or individualized training to help them get involved in sports.

The sport of triathlon was their focus and I was very impressed with them. Their Operation Rebound program, which really drew my attention, offers wounded veterans funds to get involved in triathlon. When Operation Rebound invited me to take part in their biggest event of the year, the San Diego Triathlon Challenge, I jumped at the chance. I went out to San

Diego in early 2009 to give it a go—I couldn't help but be drawn back to competition, even if this wasn't on the Paralympic level.

On the gorgeous shores of La Jolla, I was surrounded by hundreds of other athletes with physical disabilities: kids, adults, seniors, you name it. There were all ages and all abilities, all inspiring to me.

Everyone was there to give the triathlon a try, including hundreds of other amputees who looked like me. We were all drawn to one another instantly as a community of people who had similar experiences and the same goal. The triathlon itself was half an Ironman distance, and I was assigned a guide who would swim, bike, and run with me.

I hit the race hard from the beginning. Swimming the 1.2 miles in the ocean was easy under that Pacific sun. But, when I got on the bike, I struggled. I had never done fifty miles on an upright bike before, let alone up hills. This was much more difficult than the New York City Marathon. It took me hours to bike the course, and my guide had to help push me up some hills—he'd push me up, we'd take a break for me to rest, and then we would do it all over again. For fifty miles.

I didn't care. I was getting the thrill of just being out there and doing this. Because the challenge of running 13.1 miles was still a little too much, I opted to use the handcycle (which I had used in the New York City Marathon two years earlier) for the run. I knew I would eventually be able to run 13.1 miles, but not quite yet. Regardless, I crossed my first triathlon finish line beaming with pride.

This was a pivotal moment. I realized I wasn't limited to being just a swimmer, and that the triathlon might be the event that best matched my ability. I had devoted so many months to swimming, but now I was able to do three sports at once, and on the same course as people who had all their limbs. I was hooked from the moment I crossed that finish line.

This was going to be the next thing.

That triathlon wasn't a sanctioned race, but it got me hooked. I wanted to cross more finish lines. I loved the challenge of completing three different events in the same race, and I enjoyed the challenge of using different prosthetics and changing them during transitions. I couldn't wait to do another one, this time using my running leg. So much for taking a break from competitive sports—I had just fallen into a new one, and it felt like my determination had doubled.

I was a born competitor. There wasn't any way around it.

* * *

At that point, triathlon wasn't a sport contested at the Paralympic Games. There was, however, a World Championship every year. I decided that I wanted to try to qualify for the 2010 World Championships put on by the International Triathlon Union in Budapest, Hungary. I hired my first triathlon coach, Mike Durner, and spent the ensuing months swimming, biking, and running while still working full time during the day.

In order to qualify for the World Championships, I was going to have to clock a baseline time at the New York City Triathlon, which doubled as the qualifying race as well as the U.S. national championship that year.

There weren't a lot of athletes competing in paratriathlon at the time; it was a relatively new sport, and they were trying to grow it. The qualifying time, as a result, was relatively lenient. I was pretty sure I could clock it, and I did.

I flew over to Budapest myself, and Dick came over a few days later to join me and my teammates; he was well into his medical schooling by then, but he supported my triathlon training just as he had my swimming. There were eighty-five elite paratriathletes from fifteen countries racing across six different classifications, and it was going to be the biggest World Championship in the sport to date.

And the race just happened to be on September 11. That was a big deal to me, for obvious reasons. I had worn the Team USA uniform at the Paralympic Games, but now racing in the red, white, and blue on September 11 meant even more. There was a gravity to how I felt, and it deepened my resolve to do well in the race.

I lined up at the start with three other athletes who were competing in the TRI 2 category for athletes with a severe leg impairment. With paratriathlon still in its relative infancy, I thought I had a good shot at making the podium. There might have been other athletes there who could beat me, but I thought I had a real shot if I raced well.

But you always question yourself at the starting line.

That's what I did in Budapest, looking out at the open water. *Can I really win this race now that I'm here? Am I as prepared as I think I am? What if I disappoint like I did in Beijing? What if I'm not good enough to win?*

* * *

The horn went off. We battled through rainy and cold conditions in the early morning swim. Already, I could feel my training paying off. I completed that freezing swim in the Danube River and was in the lead when I got out of the water into the chilly air; I stayed in the lead during the 20K bike ride along the river's banks, hearing the wind in my ears and clicking into a groove. After that, I had a 5K around the old-world landmarks of the city. I sprinted over the beautiful Szechenyi Chain Bridge and its famous lion statues and saw the finish line in sight in the distance.

As I approached the tape, somebody on the course handed me an American flag. I knew by then that I was in first place. I grabbed the flag and raised it up over my head as I crossed my first paratriathlon World Championship finish line.

I was a world champion.

I stood on my very first international podium, awarded a gold medal while the "Star Spangled Banner" played on September 11. I closed my eyes for a moment and let the music move me, feeling that I had represented my country well. It was a moment I had been dreaming of ever since Gym Elite.

And then, when I returned home from Budapest, my world came crashing down.

Chapter 23

Shot in the Heart

It was hard to comprehend it, but Dick had become friendly with one of my teammates while we were in Budapest, and they had started something on the side. When I suspected it and called them on it, they both denied it. I chose to believe them until my teammate's husband called to let me know my suspicion had been right all along.

I felt like I had been shot in the heart. Dick and I had married young. We had started drifting apart, noticing our differences more and more. I was outgoing, he was an introvert. He was the studious type, always keeping up with current events, while I just wanted to be out doing things. It had been like that since we first started dating in Colorado. But this was a direct hit.

Dick and I decided to separate in October of 2010 and filed for a divorce. The happy marriage we had shared vanished, just like that, and was replaced by an empty feeling that I was now walking around with every day.

I would never wish divorce on anybody. I credited Dick for getting me through the toughest times of my life. He had been steady by my side through the loss of my leg and everything that came after it. He had brought me home from Iraq and slept by my side for weeks at Walter Reed. He had been there 24-7, like an angel in disguise. He had been my hero. I would never forget what he had done for me or fail to remember that part of him. I always held a lot of respect for him, and so did my parents.

I had been going to bed and waking up next to Dick for seven years. Now I was suddenly on my own with only Jake by my side, crying myself to sleep every night. It felt like I had lost more than my heart could take. Going through the divorce felt harder than losing my leg. If someone had given me the choice, I would have rather lost my leg again ten times over.

I always try to be a positive person, but I'm also a human being. I never cried nearly as much about losing my leg as I did in those first few months after separating from Dick.

One night, I drove to Target with a shopping list but ended up sitting in the car crying after I turned off the motor. I sat there for an entire hour, bawling my eyes out, unable to stop. I cried and cried and cried until I could shed no more tears. I never made it into the store.

* * *

My vulnerability at work became pretty obvious. I would burst into tears at random moments throughout the day, sometimes going into Dave's office to sit and cry. I kept wondering what my life was going to be like now.

My zest for life was still there, deep inside. I had a hard time finding it at first, but there were little glimmers as the months went on.

Having Jake around the office was like a crutch for my emotions, and we became closer than ever—he could sense my innermost feelings, and I talked and shared with him. I was going to have to restart my life, just like I had after I was injured in Iraq.

I moved into my own apartment for the first time in my life.

Is this the right thing to do? What's it going to be like being a thirty-year-old single woman?

I hadn't been single since college. I wondered if I would ever meet someone again. I had already been married to Dick when I lost my leg, so I had never had to worry about dating as an amputee. Would I ever meet someone who loved me as much as Dick did, now that I only had one leg?

* * *

One morning that December, after a couple of months of nonstop crying, continuous doubt and wondering, I woke up and realized that it was time to redefine myself and determine who I was going to be without Dick. It was time to pick myself up by the bootstraps and find the silver lining. I was going to be better off without him and life would go on. Just like when I lost my leg, this was a life-altering experience—I had come out on the other side then, and I would do it again. My marriage hadn't been what it was supposed to be, I came to realize, and it made me into someone I didn't want to be. I could move on now to pursue what I wanted to the fullest, without anything holding me back. I wasn't going to be bridled.

I chose to believe that I was going to be okay. And so, I was going to be okay.

Later that morning, I created an online dating profile on Match.com. I debated whether I should tell people upfront that I had lost my leg. I ended up not including that information, but I decided that if someone connected with me, I would tell them before we met.

Just so you know, and you're not blindsided, I'm missing one of my legs.

Then I would tell them how I lost it, and all the things I'd accomplished since then. I would show that it hadn't stopped me from doing anything I wanted. And, if someone didn't want to go out with me because of it, then that was their loss. I wouldn't want to be with them anyway. I was just as good a person as someone who had both their legs. I trusted myself, and I was proud of who I was.

I went out on all sorts of dates that month. I would honestly go out with anyone who asked me then just to get my mind off Dick. Only once did someone fail to email me back after learning that I had lost my leg. It stopped the line of communication with this one guy immediately, but everyone else wrote back with some variation of "No problem," or "See you on Tuesday." It really wasn't a big deal to them. That helped me start to return to a more normal emotional state, just believing that I could eventually find someone to share my life with again.

Five months after we separated, Dick and I finally divorced. Dick had moved away to do his medical residency, so I expected to be alone when I showed up at the courthouse. But, when I got there, he was waiting.

He had flown in to see the court proceedings through. We had been through a lot together, and it didn't end well. But the fact that he showed up that day meant a lot to me. I didn't love all the things he had done at the end of our relationship, but so much time had passed, and I had realized that I was beginning to figure out who I was without him, and I liked it.

Dick and I held hands during the entire divorce proceedings. Maybe people would think that was weird. *Who does that?* It just seemed like the right thing to do, and I think it provided positive closure for us. We had gotten married young, gone through life-changing times together, and we weren't regretful about any of it.

We stood in front of the judge together, hands locked, both agreeing to the divorce. We got the official paperwork stamped with the seal of approval.

We walked out to the parking lot together, and Dick stopped to see Jake waiting in the back seat of my car. They hadn't seen each other in months, and Jake seemed not to recognize Dick, or at least he didn't care about seeing him, and that kind of gave me a good feeling inside.

With happy tears, we said our goodbyes and sincerely wished each other the best in life and all the good luck for the future. And that was that.

That was the last time we spoke. It was as cordial a finale as it could have been. If I were to run into him now, I would genuinely hope to find him well and happy.

* * *

It was around this time that I went to a meeting at work and someone caught my eye. *Holy cow.* This guy was so good-looking. *Who is this, and why haven't I seen him before?*

The last thing on my mind was jumping into a serious relationship. My divorce had just become final. Still, I wanted to put myself out there. I found out his name was Brian, that he was from Grand Rapids, Michigan, and that he was a few months older than me.

That same month, Brian was assigned to do a rotation for his residency at the office where I worked, and he and I were working together all day, every day. He knew that I had just gone through a divorce, but there seemed to be a little flirting going on. We'd compare notes from dates that we were going on, little details that we would laugh about.

Wait, he is flirting with me, right? And I'm flirting back? What's going on?

I wondered if I was right about the way he was looking at me. He was so handsome, I figured he was out of my league. I didn't think anything could ever happen, because he was just too good for me. We were both on match.com and, one day, I got a notification that he had "winked" at me.

Is he really interested, or was that just a joke?

I was so confused, and probably started overanalyzing everything. Brian and I had been working together for almost two months when our office decided to go out for dinner and drinks together. We got to the restaurant and, in that setting, there was no denying it: There was indeed a vibe between us.

He brushed against my leg, and, for a little while, I went back into questioning whether that had been intentional or not. But, by the end of the night, I knew it had been on purpose. There was definitely a mutual interest, as our gaze lingered, and our attention focused more and more on one another.

Later, I'd find out that he'd had eyes on me the last several company meetings. He tells people he was drawn to the "bounce in my step" and my "smile that worked the room."

He took me out on our first real date in March, to a sushi restaurant. It was a scorching hot Thursday night in the city for that time of year—it felt like it was a hundred degrees out. When I got close to the restaurant, I couldn't find parking anywhere. We were supposed to meet at 6:30, but I kept having to circle the block around the place as Brian stood waiting outside.

I hate being late. It's part of having a military background. I was mortified by what was happening. Late for our first date—I couldn't stand it. I ended up parking nearly half a mile away and busted my butt to get to that sushi place as fast as I could.

I arrived drenched in sweat and had to hustle to the restroom to wring out my shirt—it was soaked through, and I refused to join Brian at the table soaking wet—and to dry my face and neck. I was embarrassed as I sat down at the table and could only imagine what I must have looked like.

Somehow, I got lucky. After that date, he was still interested in going out with me. We still laugh about our first date.

* * *

Our relationship got serious pretty quickly. My family and friends all knew how much I had gone through with my injury in Iraq and then the divorce, and they were all pretty protective of me once Brian was in the picture. They didn't want to see me get hurt again.

Brian and I were also really nervous about telling Dave about our relationship because he was both our boss and we had met at work. Dave had been such a source of support after my disappointing performance in Beijing and through the divorce—he had seen me going through some of my worst times. He was like a big brother to me, and I knew he also would not want to see me suffer again.

I told Brian it was on him to tell Dave we were dating.

One day soon after, the two of them were working on a leg together. Brian got his courage together.

"Just so you know, Dave," he blurted out. "I'm dating Melissa."

There was a receptionist in the office at the time named Melissa, who had a crush on Brian. Dave put two and two together.

"Oh, wow, that's great," he said. Dave knew that Brian had been cycling through different women at the time, finding his way through life.

Brian realized that Dave had the wrong impression.

"No, no," he said. "I'm dating Melissa Stockwell."

Dave stopped working on the leg. His expression changed. He looked Brian dead in the eyes.

"If you ever hurt her," Dave told Brian, "I will (expletive) kill you."

Chapter 24

Dare2Tri

With my personal life back on track, I was able to start focusing again on my athletic goals. Brian was a genuine, straightforward guy who was really interested in my time in the Army, my patriotic love of my country, and how much I was dedicated to sports. When we first met, he more or less thought that a triathlon was a round of golf in the afternoon, a hockey game in the evening, and a stop at the bar afterwards. Pretty quickly, he started coming to all my races and supporting me.

Our values were aligned. He got over the feeling early on that he was competing with Jake for my affection. And he recognized that my bike and my prosthetic legs were pretty much the only material things I cared about, and that loyalty means everything to me. I was over the moon to be with Brian and I started feeling that itch to set some new goals.

I started working out five times a week and competing in every local triathlon I could find. My coach recommended adding some variety to my training regimen by signing up for a spin class. I went with my friend Keri, who I had briefly met at Walter Reed a few years earlier—we were reintroduced by a mutual friend, Susan Katz (who we call Katz), who I knew from my time at the Olympic Training Center. Keri lived two blocks away, was also a triathlete, and was a thirty-year-old single woman who had also recently gone through a divorce.

As far back as when she was eight, Keri had told her dad that she had a goal of teaching people with no legs to water ski. Along with her own athletic pursuits, she had gone into working in adaptive sports. We became friends quickly and started to hang out all the time, either for workouts or at the local bar on the weekend.

My self-discipline and early morning drive came back to the surface after those months of uncertainty. I threw myself into that feeling of meeting challenges, both physical and mental, the rush of pushing through whether it was a training run or dripping sweat for ninety minutes at a time in spin class with Keri. In one of those classes, Keri and I befriended a man named Dan Tun who worked for the local park district—the three of us became a trio pretty quickly, all triathletes, all wanting to make an impact in the world through the sport.

In 2011, the three of us decided to start a nonprofit for people with disabilities to help them get started in the sport of triathlon—in the big picture, we wanted to get people with disabilities active and living healthy lives in their communities with the people they loved. Both Keri and Dan had worked in adaptive sports their entire lives, and, of course, I had my own stake in the game. The first step in getting legitimate in the industry was to obtain our USA Triathlon Level One coaching certifications. When we were at the certification training course in Madison, Wisconsin, we came up with the name Dare2Tri—it felt like something that would inspire confidence in people with disabilities.

We asked our spin instructor Stacee Seay if she would be willing to join us as our head coach. Once she was on board, Dan and Keri helped us land partnerships with the Great Lakes Adaptive Sports Association and the Chicago Park District where they respectively worked—we were creating a blend of skills and support and a network of high-quality people. This was new to all of us, so, for the first year, we set a modest goal of getting eight athletes with a physical disability to their first triathlon starting line. We got a grant from the U.S. Paralympics to help pay for everything, and our partners loaned us adaptive sports equipment to get things off the ground.

We held our first three-day Dare2Tri camp in 2012. Using word of mouth alone, we were able to recruit twenty athletes for the camp—we knew there was interest in what we were doing then because people just seemed to come out of the woodwork.

There was a need for what we were trying to create in Chicago, but we were still raw. We didn't even get T-shirts printed for that first camp, and Keri, Dan, and I weren't in a position to quit our full-time day jobs. But we all felt that this was the start of something important—I had the same feeling of possibility and camaraderie as I'd experienced in my ski trip with the Vail Veterans Program eight years before. We had coaches at the camp to help participants with their running and biking prosthetics, and we all worked together—there was a lot of encouragement and cheering one another on. Our motto became *One Inspires Many*.

We felt like we were gaining momentum. Keri, Dan, and I started visiting hospitals and schools to recruit more particpants and grow the organization. Whenever we'd encounter anyone with a physical disability, we'd tell them about Dare2Tri and invite them to try a triathlon. People might have thought we were crazy until we described the coaching and resources, we had put together for anyone who wanted to push their limits.

One day, we drove nearly a hundred miles to a hospital in Rockford, Illinois, to put on a triathlon clinic at a park district recreation center. We had called in advance to let the hospital staff know we were coming and to invite them to come check it out. It was there that I met a nine-year-old kid named Jack who had a big personality—his spirit was amazing. I think I saw something of my younger self in him from the first time we met.

Jack had lost one leg just two months before. It hadn't formed correctly and had been a problem all his life, so he made the tough choice to have it amputated. Jack showed up at the clinic with his dad, his brother Max and sister Mia. I found out that his mother, Heidi, hadn't come because she was angry with her husband for bringing Jack to the clinic—she was struggling with the sight of her son on crutches, and couldn't fathom him trying a triathlon within the new reality ahead of him. Jack had been a phenomenal swimmer before he lost his leg, and his mom was worried about giving him false hope—this was her way of protecting him in such a difficult moment.

I watched Jack that day as he swam and got into the handcycle and the racing chair that he would use until he could learn to run on a prosthetic. I noticed his potential and fire right away. It wasn't as though things were coming easy for him, but he had the determination to move fast and push through limits.

At the end of the clinic, I got out of the water and wrapped a towel around me. I bent down to eye level with this fiery nine-year-old.

"You can be a champion," I told him.

He looked up at me, and I saw belief in his eyes.

Sometimes people just need to hear the words. *You can do this.*

Some people take that kind of encouragement to heart and some don't. Jack did. He chose to believe in what I was saying and to believe in himself. He took up triathlon after that day— literally taking my advice and running with it. I'm still currently Jack's triathlon coach, and Brian makes his prosthetic legs. His family lives a few miles from us and his mom, Heidi, who once had her doubts, is now his biggest cheerleader. I have no doubt that Jack is going to be a Paralympian someday. I feel a profound honor that I have played a part in evoking that power of choice in him.

Sports changed my life after I lost my leg. I wanted to use athletics to help others in the same situation to find self-confidence and self-worth, to have that feeling of crossing the finish line under their own power.

Ask someone you know if they want to do a triathlon—the answer is almost always no. And, if you ask someone with a disability, the chance of getting a yes is even smaller.

I wanted to change that. I knew I could give people hope. Maybe not everyone would think it was their thing, but I could point the way to the empowerment of stepping up to the starting line and start changing their lives. If even one person felt that kind of power, then Dare2Tri was going to be a win.

That alone would make me feel like I've lived a successful life.

If you can impact one person's life for the better and open up possibility and show them what they're capable of, then that's the biggest victory of all.

* * *

The same summer I met Jack, I returned to Landstuhl for the first time since losing my leg. I went with the Wounded Warrior Project as part of their Resilience Program, and I had the opportunity to say thank you to all of the hospital staff who had helped me with my recovery. The doctors, nurses, and staff there had seen me at the absolute lowest point of my life—the week after the roadside bomb and the days that followed. Everyone there did their jobs incredibly well, and they had never gotten to see what became of me.

One of the doctors told me that he was surprised to see me alive. He told me he didn't think I would make it.

I walked through the white-walled hospital wards and saw the process of offloading newly injured soldiers. I got into the flight line and said thank you and good luck to the dozens of newly injured personnel there who were headed stateside to Walter Reed.

Those nurses and doctors at Landstuhl were totally invested in the newly injured soldiers. They lived and breathed hope for every single one of us, doing everything they could to make us feel safe and comfortable.

When I was flying back to the United States, I felt such a powerful sense of the wonderful life I was living. And I reminded myself to live it to the fullest for those who no longer can, and for those who had saved my life during those dark days, years before.

* * *

My life is one full of inspiration. Inspiring others like Jack, feeling inspired by the work of the staff at Landstuhl—it all gave me even more drive to continue competing in triathlons. My next goal was to make the next team competing in the World Championship.

I placed first or second in my classification in most of the Paratriathlon races I competed in. When I finished, I tried to always be carrying an American flag overhead to represent my inspiration. Standing on the winner's podium listening to "The Star Spangled Banner," I never failed to feel goosebumps.

In 2011, I flew back to Beijing to compete in my second Paratriathlon World Championships. It was my first time back in that amazing city since my failure at the Water Cube.

It was also the first time I had been back since Jimi had tragically passed away in a mountain climbing accident—I'll never forget finishing a local 5K in Chicago and getting a phone call that filled me with shock and so much sadness, knowing I would never see his smile again. I was going to dedicate my race to him. He had pushed me to new limits and had never stopped believing in me for a single moment. It was hard to remember how I had let him down, and I remembered how he hugged and supported me even after a terrible race. I was going to cross the finish line in Beijing holding an American flag, no matter where I placed and flashing Jimi's signature peace sign as high as I could. I knew he'd be looking down on me with that big smile on his face that had warmed my heart so many times.

It is what it is, Jimi.

I arrived at the race site two hours in advance, still on a sugar high from the bag of gummy worms I had eaten the night before. While I was getting ready, I kept asking myself whether I should wear my wetsuit—the water temperature was a boiling eighty degrees. I decided not to, which would probably shave the minute off my time that it took me to shed it during transition.

The swim felt good. I thought about Jimi's voice calling out from the pool deck while I completed it and came out of the water first. I was efficient and focused as I put on my bike leg.

I was a little nervous about the two-loop 22K bike course. It was the hilliest and most technical ride I'd ever tackled, and hills aren't my thing.

It started with a total killer of a hill. I hit it hard but probably was only going about five miles an hour—not exactly a confidence builder.

The ride was a struggle. By the time I got to the eight-lap run, the competition had nearly caught up with me. I felt a brief moment of panic rising up inside me. *Can I do this?*

I decided that this was my race to win, as I set out on the 5K run around a gorgeous set of grandstands. I let the sound of the crowd and the feeling of the air settle me. Because we were on a loop, I could keep an eye on my competition. At every turn, I would gauge my place in the race.

Around the final turn, I felt as good as I ever had. My body pulsed with heat as I ran a personal best. I knew that the world title was mine.

Nearing the finish line, I was handed an American flag. I held it up high as I crossed the finish line, pumping peace signs in the air all the while.

The race had been close—I won by just under a minute. I also led the U.S. team to a podium sweep while gaining my second consecutive world title.

I beamed with pride and felt that I had redeemed the hurt and the doubt of failure that had filled me after the Water Cube. I stood to represent my country, to represent the wounded soldiers, to honor the memories of those who couldn't be there.

From that day forward, I would eat a full bag of gummy worms the night before a big race. I like to think that sweet tooth I'd had since I was a kid had been advantageous to me after all.

Chapter 25

Commander-in-Chief

I kept pushing. The next World Championships were a year out, but I had another item I needed to check off my list: the New York City Marathon. I had completed it with a handcycle, but, this time, I ran it on a prosthetic leg.

It was tough. If you've ever run a marathon, you know how each mile can start to feel like five. But the beautiful city and the crowd cheering us runners on kept me going. My friend, Jen, lived in New York City and knew how to get around quickly. She got Brian and Jake exactly where they needed to be, and I saw them four or five times over the course of those 26.2 miles. I managed a triumphant smile as I hobbled across the finish line with my friends Becca and Marc who had run by my side.

The experience gave me an extra edge in the running segment of the next Paratriathlon World Championships, which were in Auckland, New Zealand. The swim part of the race was shortened that day from 750 meters to 300 because the water temperature was less than sixty degrees—we're talking ice-cream-headache cold. This really worried me, because I always counted on a strong swim being the strength of my triathlon.

But as a friend once said: *It is what it is.*

I finished the tooth-chattering swim. Then I managed my best bike splits ever and ended up with a solid run down the finish chute holding the American flag high as I crossed the finish line with a little dance.

I'd completed a three-peat of world titles. That championship feeling never gets old.

* * *

When I wasn't training or looking ahead to the next race, I was still working with the wounded veteran population. That year I was one of nineteen veterans, and the only woman headed for the 100-kilometer mountain bike ride President George W. Bush held every year. I'd eventually be invited two times, once riding in Amarillo at Palo Dura State Canyon and the following year at his ranch in Crawford, TX.

The three-day event is called the W100 and is actually organized by my former Commander-in-Chief. I was a little hesitant about it—I'd never really mountain biked before, even when I had two legs. The distance of sixty miles also seemed daunting. But it wasn't a challenge that I was going to turn down, so I borrowed a friend's bike and flew there.

I have so many unforgettable memories from those two rides. The President's ranch house was so surreal. There were pictures of him everywhere with famous people, such as the Pope and the Dalai Lama. I was pretty much in awe of the chance to meet him after I'd missed his visit to Walter Reed years before.

He was very down to earth. In the morning, he came out to shake all the veterans' hands and we stood together listening to the national anthem with our hands on our hearts. We all saddled up on our bikes on the mountain trails. The scenery was stark and gorgeous.

As we started the ride, every so often, I would look off in the distance and spot what, at first, I thought were treehouses. As I got closer, I realized that these little huts were posts for Secret Service agents posted with weapons along the route.

The ride was difficult. We tackled steep rocky inclines and rode over bridges that spanned the whole canyon. I was an inexperienced, one-legged mountain biker, and it was a tough one for me. But the comradeship among the veterans was incredible. Some of the volunteer bikers would ride ahead of me, then jump off when I got there and actually help push me up the hill before jumping back on their saddles to resume the ride. That first day, the riders who helped me up the hills called themselves Team Melissa, as we had a friendly rivalry with Team Dan pushing another amputee up the steepest hills.

President Bush made it a point to ride with every single veteran every day. He would always bring a light spirit and entertainment to the ride and helped me mentally and physically on those hills. On a slope heading up, I was pushing into the breeze, working hard with the sun overhead when I sensed someone trailing me. I glanced back to see the President in his sunglasses, keeping pace with me.

"Atta boy...girl!" he called out in encouragement. "That's what I'm talking about!"

Every night at his ranch, we'd have a wonderful dinner with the President, along with a celebratory event. On the last night, there was a concert in the living room of his house on the ranch. I was sitting next to the Bushes when the band kicked into the song, "Oh Happy Day." From their reactions, I could tell it was one they obviously enjoyed—they were both bobbing their heads to the beat in their seats.

Another time, a country band was playing an outdoor concert when I jokingly leaned over to the President. "Would you like to dance?" I asked him.

"Oh, no. No, thank you," he replied.

A couple of minutes went by, and another veteran came to the table and asked Laura Bush if she wanted to dance with him. She agreed and got up immediately.

President Bush then turned and looked at me; he held out his hand.

I felt like I was dancing with my dad. As the band played, President Bush twirled me around in front of a line of cameras that was capturing the moment. He was wearing sneakers and a plaid shirt; I danced along, pinching myself and wondering if this was really happening

It was amazing. Here I was, sharing a dance with the President who had been Commander-in-Chief when I lost my leg. I never wanted to be injured in combat, and he never wanted to see the wounds that his decisions had caused. But it happened, and now we were dancing together.

Later on, our dance that evening was the subject of one of the portraits he painted in his book, *Portraits of Courage*, which was his tribute to American military veterans.

I got to know President Bush as a person during that trip, and I learned what an incredible human being he is. Not only is he witty and fun, a great athlete, and a fine dancer, but, politics aside, he's held himself accountable for the decisions he made while he was President. He understands and owns how his decisions affected people's lives, including those lives that were lost and those whose lives were severely altered—like mine. He's chosen to accept those consequences and to honor those of us who are here and those who are not. In my mind, President or not, that's the making of a great man.

I left Texas on such a high, along with a few bruises and the memory of what cactus felt like in my posterior. It kept me light as a feather for weeks, feeling like I was the luckiest girl alive.

* * *

In April of 2013, President Bush invited me back to Texas to recite the Pledge of Allegiance at the dedication of his Presidential Library in College Station. I accepted in a heartbeat and flew with my parents to attend what was a truly grand ceremony.

When we arrived, everyone was escorted to their seats, except those of us who were going to be taking the stage. It was about a half-hour before things were getting underway, and a woman took me aside and escorted me to an empty room to wait.

There was a lot of bustling as people were preparing, and it felt strange to be sitting there all alone. I could hear the thousands of people gathering outside, voices talking, commotion everywhere. There I was, standing on a cold marble floor in a long room and staring at white walls lined with the names of the donors who had contributed to building the library.

I was starting to get nervous. *What's going on? Did they forget about me?*

Suddenly, a huge line of serious-looking Secret Service men with radios in their ears and an attitude that showed they were all-business came into the room. A moment later, I realized why, as they were followed by all five living Presidents and their wives.

Barack Obama. Bill Clinton. George Bush. Jimmy Carter. George W. Bush.

I froze against the wall like a mannequin. I tried to will myself to be invisible and not get in anyone's way.

George W. Bush, in a black suit and blue-checkered tie, spotted me and caught my eye. I saw him glance down at my prosthetic leg decorated with the American flag as he waved at me and interrupted the conversations going on around him.

"Let me introduce you to my friend, Melissa," he said.

All of the Presidents and their wives came over and circled around me. The Secret Service formed a half-circle ring behind them. I was introduced to everybody, one by one.

President Bush told everyone about me and my story, and how we had met during the ride at his ranch. I was almost speechless as I managed to say, "Nice to meet you, Mister President," over and over. I felt like I was in a dream. As the circle dispersed to get back to preparing for the event, President Obama paused to ask me how my life in Chicago was going and about the progress of Dare2Tri. I had no idea how he knew about these things, but we spoke, just the two of us, for a few minutes.

"I'm proud of you," he finally said, getting one of his presidential coins out of his pocket as a gift. President Bush was standing close by, and he put his arm around me as he cracked a joke to put everyone at ease. I noticed Condoleezza Rice had come in and was standing on the opposite end of the room practicing pronouncing the names of all the foreign dignitaries in attendance.

It had to be the most surreal moment of my life.

I felt like I was exuding pure patriotism, just being in that room with those people. On that day, political views didn't matter—what was important was that several of our country's leaders had come together to honor one of their peers, and, by extension, America itself. I had never been prouder to be American.

When the ceremony began, all five First Ladies filed out onto the stage followed by the Presidents. I came behind them, walking onto the stage in my bright white dress, American flag scarf, and American flag prosthetic leg as the color guard passed me by. I took my place stage left, the orchestra pit behind me silenced as the announcer introduced me to the thousands of distinguished guests in the rows of seats below the stage.

It was nerve-wracking. I was on stage with all the living Presidents, and the ceremony was being broadcast around the country. I had said the Pledge of Allegiance probably a thousand times in my life, but never like this.

I spotted my parents in the second row of the audience, right next to President Obama's daughters. I put my hand over my heart, and with confidence began to recite the Pledge. I remembered every word perfectly, and the crowd started to join me about halfway through.

I finished and started walking down the stairs to my seat; I couldn't stop smiling and felt like I was glowing from inside. As I made my way into the audience, I heard President Bush yelling something from the stage.

"Atta girl!" he hollered, winking and smiling.

Chapter 26

Iron Woman

I flew to my fourth Paratriathlon World Championships in London hoping to claim a fourth straight title. One of my main competitors this time around was going to be Hailey Danz—a former Dare2Tri summer intern. Hailey had lost her leg to bone cancer when she was fourteen, and, before she was offered the internship, Keri made her promise to try a triathlon. I was there to teach her how to clip her prosthetic leg into her bike during the transition at her first race. She was a natural, and I had been beside her as she made a quick ascent onto the world stage. We competed together the year before at my third World Championships in New Zealand, where I took the top spot for my third championship, but Hailey had gotten much faster since then and I knew it would be a battle for first.

The race was on Friday the 13th in Hyde Park and—naturally—it was wet and rainy. I had a strong swim and was the first out of the water, but a mile into the second loop of the bike course something started to feel strange every time I pushed the pedal.

Then I heard it. *Flap, flap, flap.*

I looked down and there it was—a flat tire. I'd never suffered a flat during a race, much less at the World Championships. I panicked. I yelled out that I had a flat but kept pedaling—I was caught off guard and didn't know what to do. I couldn't top more than ten miles per hour during that third loop, which was ridiculous.

This was the World Championships. I kept yelling and looked up at the crowd, hoping someone would intervene. Brian called out to tell me that Keri was waiting in the wheel pit. I crept my way there, where she helped me switch out the entire wheel.

We also realized that my front brakes were broken. But what would I need to brake for?

I got back on the course to complete the final three loops, having no idea where I stood in the pack as I tried to make up for lost time. When I approached the dismount line at the end of the last loop, I pulled the brakes and—of course—nothing happened. I pulled harder. I slid past the line and managed to come to a full stop as I saw a red flag being raised out of the corner of my eye.

Turns out the officials take the dismount line very seriously. A penalty it would be.

Somehow, after all this drama, I was still in second place. Only one competitor, from Denmark, was ahead of me. I struggled to get my running leg on quickly, but the damp silicon liner wasn't working well with my hands wet from sweat. I finally got it on and sprinted into a run, seeing Hailey dismounting her bike just behind me.

I was about 1.5 miles into the run when I heard the unmistakable sound of someone running with a prosthetic leg behind me. Intuitively, I knew it was Hailey, and she was pulling up on my right.

I tried to stay with her, but she was on fire. I kept her in sight for the remainder of the run, but my flat tire, weakening leg, and looming penalty got to me—I was mentally frail and unable to catch her. A few hundred feet before the finish, I saw my number posted in the penalty box. That meant I had to stop, dart into it, and wait ten seconds. Then I got out and was able to run to Brian to grab my American flag from him, so I'd have it for my signature crossing of the finish line.

It was bittersweet. It hadn't been my race, but the Danish competitor ended up with a disqualifying penalty and Hailey was given the gold. Hailey had the best race of her life.

Had I wanted to win that day? *Absolutely.* But seeing Hailey beat me for her first world title just more than two years after I helped Dave fit her for her first running leg—it was incredible.

Just like on April 13, 2004, things weren't always in my control. It is what it is.

And, hey, I thought, sprinkling some silver into my collection of gold was going to add some color. Nothing wrong with that. I even took my flat tire home with me and put it in my room as a reminder that not everything in life is going to be perfect.

* * *

Luckily, I had another race coming up seven weeks later to keep me motivated—an Ironman. I was going to swim 2.4 miles, bike 112 miles, then run 26.2 miles. That's 140.6 miles in total. You get seventeen hours to complete it. *And* people pay to do this!

The Ironman is the pinnacle of all triathlons. In the triathlon community, completing one puts you in the "cool kids" club. It's not for the faint of heart. I had signed up the year before and had been training longer distances, waking Brian up far too many times as I rose to train at five in the morning and tried to sneak out without waking him. He'd heard me talking about it endlessly, and he gave me encouragement—he understood how much I needed to keep looking for things to challenge and inspire me.

When we arrived at Tempe, Arizona, for the race, I felt kind of like I did when I got to Iraq in 2004—I hadn't processed how immense of a challenge this was going to be until I was actually there. A few mornings later, a 4:20 wake-up call shot me up and out of bed before the sun came up. I gathered with about 2,500 other nervous racers in the dark and got my armed marked with my number, 127, in black Sharpie.

I got quick pep talks from Brian and Keri, along with Katz (both Ironwomen themselves)—they were all there to cheer me on, along with my parents, who had surprised me with their presence the day before. I got into the water right on time at 6:45, and then a cannon went off and I set out to swim into the first wave.

I was speeding along through mild water past a series of buoys, eventually clocking a solid time of 1:07 that I was pleased with. Keri and Brian helped me out of the water and I gave my parents a quick hug as I ran to transition. The crowd was roaring encouragement and I was smiling ear to ear as I removed my wetsuit, threw on my biking leg, and headed out for the ridiculously long 112-mile bike ride that lay ahead.

Thanks to the help of a tailwind, I averaged 15.2 miles per hour on the three-loop bike course—the cheers of familiar faces along the course helped, along with a peanut butter and jelly sandwich and some chocolate chip cookies that I scarfed down on the second lap.

When I got off the bike after that epic ride, I changed my clothes and even brushed my teeth during the transition to getting ready for the run—I wanted to feel fresh, and my excitement burned through the fatigue. Still, as I started the run, I could feel a throat spasm coming on. This had happened before—it's an issue that can arise when I over-exert myself or get too excited. It makes it hard to swallow, which leads to repercussions such as problems with eating, drinking, and breathing. I was determined not to let it stop me—I had already gone too far, and I dug deep and focused my mind on taking the rest of the race step by step.

I started slowly in the first of two 13.1 mile loops around the lake, trying to feel my legs again after the long bike ride. I kept thinking my body would kick in and my pace would pick up. But it didn't. I couldn't get any food in me at the water stops other than a few grapes. Keri jumped in the run with me for part of the way, and I saw Brian on the sidelines making funny faces to pick me up—as the run went on, he even ran back to the hotel to get Jake and held my dog in his arms trying to get me to laugh. I think Brian ran a marathon himself that day trying to keep in contact with me.

My friend and fellow wounded soldier, Dan, another spectator surprise, called out at one point: "From Walter Reed to Ironman! You got this, Stockwell!"

Did I?

By the time I reached the halfway point, the sun had gone down. I looked around; I was running all alone in the dark, holding glowsticks that the volunteers had given me. It was hard to keep track of time. I was pretty miserable.

I managed a smile when Katz joined me for a while on my second running loop. I dug deeper, keeping a steady rhythm, trying to blend my will with the motion, but I started going even further downhill as I passed mile twenty.

My leg burned with blisters. I began to question everything.

I can't believe I actually paid to do this. Why am I paying to suffer? This is horrible. Everything hurts.

By then, I was crying silent tears as faces passed me by and that moment was a deep low.

But that's why you signed up for this, Melissa.

To get to the lowest of the low and find out what happens next: that's the point. I dug deep. And I came to the realization that I was out there running for those who couldn't run, and for those who had made the ultimate sacrifice. That thought kept me going.

One foot in front of the other.

I played the game of breaking down the run into one light pole to the next. Pain came and went. Finally, I could see Dan holding an American flag, waiting for me at mile twenty-six. He passed it to me as I rounded a corner with two-tenths of a mile to go.

The finish line: I could see it. My friends and family were there screaming their lungs out under the bright lights. Suddenly, I could run again. After fifteen long hours, I felt like I was floating.

It was a blur. I crossed the finish line and heard the announcement: "Melissa Stockwell, you are an Ironman!"

I finished the entire race in fifteen hours and twelve minutes. I stood at the finish line feeling an entire ocean of emotion as my loved ones surrounded me. Brian ran up and put the medal around my neck. My parents, Keri, and Katz gave me celebratory hugs.

We hailed a pedicab to get back to our hotel. It was going to take a little while to recover, but all I kept thinking was: the human body and mind are capable of so much more than we give them credit for. It takes digging deeper than you ever imagined you could, but there are amazing things on the other side.

* * *

My relationship with Brian was getting serious, and I returned home keen to focus more on my personal life. Things felt right, and I knew he was the one I wanted to be with and the one that I would marry someday. Lucky for me, the feeling was mutual, and Brian was my biggest supporter as I pursued my restless dreams.

Then came the big breakthrough: Triathlon was announced as a new official sport for the upcoming 2016 Paralympic Games in Rio. That immediately fell into place as my next goal. But I also understood that Brian and I were getting a little older, and we wanted to start a family—this meant starting to plan our future. We sat down with a calendar—literally—to map out when I'd have to get pregnant in order to still have enough time to recover, come back, and train for the Paralympics.

The path was clear: I needed to get pregnant between December 2013 and March 2014. I would need to have the baby by the end of 2014 to have time to get back into peak shape to make Rio a possibility. If that didn't happen, then a baby would have to wait until after the games. We were going to do whatever we could to make sure I was at the starting line of the triathlon in Rio.

That winter, on Brian's birthday, we signed off on buying a duplex in Chicago and moved in together. I turned the key to unlock the door for the first time, and, when I walked in, I got a surprise—there was an elaborate picnic set up and waiting for us on the floor of the empty house.

Brian got down on one knee. "Will you marry me?" he asked.

Me? Marry this handsome guy?

I couldn't believe it. He was so genuine, always so supportive. He made me laugh, and he made me feel like the most beautiful girl in the world. I said yes without hesitating. I couldn't wait to share the news; my family and my close friends would be just as excited, and I knew they would love the idea of me and him being together forever.

Chapter 27

The Mommy Road to Rio

February came and went. Then March. Then April. I still wasn't pregnant.

It wasn't going to happen before Rio. The window had passed, so we stopped trying.

April wasn't bad, though. We celebrated Little Leg's tenth birthday—a huge milestone—with a big bash at Six Degrees. This was our favorite neighborhood bar, and it was always a place that made us feel good and welcome.

Little Leg was growing up so fast. That year's slogan for Little Leg's birthday was *A Decade to Remember*. There was a lot of drinking and dancing. I had a lot of deep emotion—so much had happened since that day in Iraq. I had met some of my best friends since then, as well as my soon-to-be husband—all of whom had only known me as someone with one leg.

To say that life was good would be an understatement.

But the week after the big bash, I didn't feel well. Something wasn't right. I was exhausted all the time. I was constantly starving and couldn't get full. I thought that maybe I was anemic again like had happened after I lost my leg, so I called my doctor to order some blood work.

Keri, who was pregnant at the time, jokingly said that she was tired of my complaining—so she urged me to take a pregnancy test.

"I'm not pregnant," I told her.

But, three days before my appointment for the blood work, I had my doubts. I took a test, and the result came back positive. Keri was right, I was going to have a baby. I must have gotten pregnant in March at the very end of the window I'd set for myself. I went to the doctor and got the result confirmed.

Brian and I were going to be parents. We shared so many mixed emotions: excitement, fear, joy, doubt. All of it. Sometimes, I felt like I could barely take care of myself, so how was I going to be totally responsible for someone else? Plus, this was going to be an issue if I was going to compete in the next Paralympics. The baby was due in January 2015, and I'd really have to accelerate my training if I wanted to be in shape to compete in Rio. Looking back, in the grand scheme of things, it seems almost silly to be so focused on my training when we were having a baby—but that's where my attention was in the moment.

I continued to train as much as I could, believing that the fitter I could be through the pregnancy, the less time it would take to come all the way back after giving birth. My next big race was at the end of May in Texas, and I thought it would be okay to compete while being just seven weeks along. But the day before I was scheduled to fly to Texas, I woke up to a lot of bleeding and freaked out. *Was I going to lose the baby?*

Brian drove me right to the emergency room, where they performed my first ultrasound. As the procedure got started, the doctor's eyes got really big. Brian was also looking at the screen, and he had a strange expression on his face.

I couldn't help but laugh nervously. "Is everything okay?" I asked.

The doctor paused and smiled. "Yes," he reassured me. "But I think you're a little farther along than seven weeks."

Come to find out, I was actually fourteen weeks pregnant—already in my second trimester. Somehow, I'd gotten pregnant back in January and gone three whole months without realizing it. I was due in November. Of course, my first thought then was that this meant I'd have more time to come back and train before Rio.

As a thirty-four-year-old woman, I didn't understand how I didn't know I was pregnant for three months, but I had definitely cruised through that first trimester. My baby had already been on a trip to the Napa vineyards, skiing in Colorado, and danced on a bar for Little Leg's birthday. Everything was going to work out. It was fun to call my friends and family and let them know the baby was coming a few *months* earlier than we had previously thought.

I didn't end up racing in Texas that week, but we still flew down there to cheer on my teammates. Brian and I were that cliché couple on the plane, making up for lost time by busily reading through *What to Expect When You're Expecting* and *What to Expect When Your Wife is Expanding*. If Jake could read, he would have a copy of *What to Expect When a Little Human Comes Along*.

* * *

Brian and I were doing things a little backwards. We first bought a house, then we were going to have a baby and then decided that we'd get married after the baby was born—I didn't want to be pregnant at my wedding, and I wanted some time to lose any baby weight, so I could fit into a wedding dress. Once I found out that I was due in November, we set our wedding date for May of 2015.

With the help of my coach Stacee, I kept training as much as I could throughout my pregnancy, and I was able to compete in the Chicago triathlon in August. My doctor allowed me to race but I had to keep my heart rate below 150; I wore a monitor throughout the race and Keri helped me in the transitions. We were quite a sight for the spectators: one pregnant woman helping another pregnant woman check her heart monitor while putting on her prosthetic leg and clipping onto a bike.

I got cheers from the crowd: *Go Mama!* I tried to suck in my belly but was unsuccessful. I made it to the finish, but, by the end, I realized that I had tried to go a lot faster than I should have and that my heart rate had gotten too high. It was hard to turn off that instinct for competition, but that would be my last race before the baby was born and a new chapter in life began.

* * *

Dallas Patrick Tolsma was born on November 25, 2014, at seven pounds, ten ounces. He was named after Brian's grandfather and father, and he didn't come as expected.

I had planned out a natural delivery, but the doctors determined during the long delivery that my pelvis was too narrow to deliver a baby that way. I cried when they told me I needed a C-section after trying to push the baby out for hour after painful hour. This was going to mean a longer and more difficult recovery before I could train again—I'd need six weeks off instead of four, and, in my mind, every week mattered. This was exactly what I had been trying to avoid. I went into the surgery exhausted and unhappy but realizing that this was the only way he was going to get out into the world. I was totally preoccupied with training.

Dallas changed my life from the moment he came out. I had thought my heart was full, and that I knew how much love I had in it, but a whole new world of love blossomed and opened up inside me. I couldn't believe he was mine, this little baby with this tiny scrunched-up face and a hand that barely wrapped around my pinkie finger. But he was mine. I would be his momma forever, and I was enamored with him. I had so much love for him that I thought my heart was going to burst. Suddenly, my timeline for getting back to training wasn't as important.

He had to spend a few days in the NICU because I had a fever during the delivery and he had a little trouble breathing on his own at first. The C-section had also wreaked havoc on my body, and I couldn't wear my prosthetic for a few days afterward. I had to push myself in my wheelchair down to the NICU every few hours to feed him. I hadn't used a wheelchair since my days at Walter Reed, but now I needed one to see my baby. It was worth every ounce of effort.

Being a mom was now the most important job in my life, but I still wanted to try to make Rio a reality. At six weeks, the doctor cleared me to return to training. I quickly realized that trying to get back into elite-level shape was going to be almost as hard as returning to athletics after losing my leg. Everything was difficult, harder than I had imagined. Running again was the toughest. I started out walking, then jogging for a minute, then jogging in four-minute intervals with walking in between. My fitness wasn't going to come back overnight. It took a full six to eight months until I felt like myself again. I learned quickly that I had to take things a little at a time and reward myself by celebrating small successes along the way.

I can still remember the first time I ran a mile without stopping after I had Dallas. It was a slow mile, but I didn't care. *I ran a mile!*

Of course, I also had the typical new-mom challenges of feeling like I never got to sleep and figuring out a million little things, and I wanted to be there for Dallas as much as possible. Going to Rio was still a major goal, but it slipped down to the second tier.

In reality, my entire perspective on life had changed. Before my son, triathlon was pretty much everything. If I missed a workout, I would let it get me down. I would fixate on thinking that that missed workout would be the difference in qualifying for a race or not or making the podium or being left out. But, when I returned to training after having Dallas, I'd feel okay if I missed a workout or if I had a bad training session. There was a lot more to live for. When I got home, I would see my little baby, and I would know that everything was okay.

* * *

While I was taking the time to have a baby, all of my competitors were getting faster—so now I was playing catch-up. Some mornings, I'd wake up, look over at the baby monitor, and ponder whether I should go to Dallas for a long cuddle. But then I'd look at the sticky note I left on my nightstand. It said: *Rio 2016.*

Instead, I'd jump out of my bed and go to the pool for practice. While I brushed my teeth, I'd read another sticky note on the mirror: *You got this.*

Still, there were mornings when I would ask myself: *Why am I doing this?* I'd get up before the sun and have to miss waking up Dallas in the morning because I was already at the pool training. I was missing out on spending time with him because I wanted to make this Paralympic dream happen.

But I came to realize that just because I had a kid didn't mean that I should stop chasing those dreams. In the long run, competing in Rio would make me happier and more fulfilled, and I wouldn't have lingering questions about what could have been. When Dallas got older, he would realize that his mom went for those dreams and didn't let them go. So I kept on training, and it made me appreciate the time I spent with him even more.

* * *

My first race back after childbirth was in March of 2015, only four months after having a baby, and my times were horrible. Still, it felt good to be back on a triathlon course. I smiled the whole race, just savoring the energy and the motion, and Brian was there at the finish line holding Dallas—a first for the three of us.

That day, I definitely felt a renewed love for triathlon and proved that I could be both a mom and a competitive athlete. Around this time, I started getting asked a lot about how I balanced everything: being an elite athlete, a mom, the co-founder of a nonprofit. The answer came pretty simply. With everything that's happened in my life, I've learned to focus on what and who I'm the most passionate about—and then care for those people and make those things happen. There's always time to do the things you really want to do—and there are also always excuses close at hand. Whether it's kids or chores or setbacks in life, those things will always be there. If you want to do something badly enough, you'll stop using those as excuses and find a way to do it. That's what I did, and you can do it too. There is a way.

* * *

On May 8, 2015, Brian and I had a fairytale wedding. As any bride will surely tell you, our wedding was definitely the best. The morning of our wedding, I took all my bridesmaids—some military veterans—for a run along the Chicago waterfront. We sang cadences together, just like I had during my time in the Army. We all still laugh about the looks we got from the other runners.

That night, we had the wedding in a big historic building that had a rustic feel, even though it was in the heart of bustling Chicago. The city skyline was the backdrop for pictures, along with a scenic bridge over a big lagoon. The night was everything I imagined it could be. Jake did his duty by carrying the rings down the aisle for us. Dallas, six months old, was pulled down the aisle in a wagon. I walked down the aisle with my dad, with a little American flag patch sewed inside my wedding dress as my mom watched with tears in her eyes. Two of my Army friends in dress uniforms carried a large American flag down the aisle while a bagpipe played "Amazing Grace" and we paid our respects to those who weren't with us anymore. Brian and I then folded the flag and placed it in a special box we'd made for that day. We keep that flag in our house as both a wedding memento and a way to remember with respect those who couldn't make it to our wedding.

The wedding reception was set in dazzling candlelight, as Brian and I spent hours on the dancefloor celebrating our new lives together. The night ended with all of us begging the band to play "Proud to Be an American" as an encore and a perfect end to the night.

Eight of my fellow veterans attended the wedding in all, including five of whom had been wounded, and we gathered in an inner circle as the other guests crowded around us. Together, we belted out "Proud to Be an American" as loud and clear as we possibly could.

* * *

Our honeymoon included a trip to Japan, so I could compete in a triathlon, and then we finished up with a few days in Hawaii. We had a laugh that I somehow fit a quick triathlon into our honeymoon week. But, by then, my focus was shifted heavily to a training routine that would get me to Rio.

The World Championships that summer happened to be in Chicago—this was the race where I hoped to prove that I was all the way back. On competition day, I woke up to thunder and lightning, and I was nervous that the swim—still my strongest part of the race—might be canceled. But I was in luck; the storm tapered off, and I came out of the water with a thirteen-second lead and one of my best swims since Dallas.

I was passed during the cycling portion by a competitor from Finland. Then, as I came into transition and got off my bike to put on my running leg, the belt on my prosthetic leg broke. I couldn't believe it. The belt is designed to wrap around my waist and keep the leg from rotating while I run. I could still manage a running stride, but, every few steps, I would have to twist the leg back out. I ended up holding onto the belt with one hand and trying to hold it tight—it made for the most awkward running style, although I regained my lead for a while.

My teammate, Allysa Seely sprinted past me midway through the run, and then Hailey caught up with me as well, as I rounded the iconic Buckingham Fountain in downtown Chicago. I ran in perfect unison with Hailey—my training partner, mentee, and Dare2Tri teammate—in our hometown for about half a mile, while I did my best to hold onto that belt and keep my leg from spinning on me.

As we got closer to the finish, Hailey passed me with all of our friends cheering from the sidelines. I finished third for our first American sweep at the podium—and we all finished within a minute and three seconds of each other. It was a pretty good showing for my first World Championships after having a baby—and while pulling a busted belt the whole way.

* * *

Now Allysa, Hailey, and I were all ranked in the top ten in the world. But I was going to be the third American in line—within every paratriathlon classification, only two athletes from each country could qualify for the Paralympics. If it was possible for three to compete, it would only be by special invitation. In all likelihood, I was either going to have to surpass Allysa or Hailey in the rankings the following year or hope I would be awarded one of the special discretionary slots by the ITU.

I raced a few other times in early 2016 under the direction of my new coaches Jen and Liz, and I never did beat Hailey or Allysa—although I did well enough to be ranked in the world top five. I thought: *If I'm ranked top five, how could they not invite me to compete in Rio?*

In June, the 2016 U.S. Paratriathlon team was announced. My name wasn't on the list. But I knew that the discretionary invitation slots had yet to be awarded, and I was hoping this would be my ticket. The next two months of waiting to find out was an awkward time. I kept training like I was going to Rio, even though I didn't know if it was really going to happen or not.

I knew that I was going to get a phone call on July 8 from USA Triathlon team manager Amanda Duke—the phone was going to ring with either good news or bad. I was spending that week at my parents' house in South Carolina for our Fourth of July get-together.

I woke up that day and there was a tangible tension in the air for all of us, from me and Brian to my parents to my sister and her kids. Even Jake could sense it. Everyone I knew was aware that I was waiting for the call that day. We were excited. We were nervous. I was trying to prepare for being either devastated or ecstatic—there wasn't going to be much in between.

Tired of rattling around the house, by nine in the morning, all of us were getting our things together to head for the lake when my phone rang. This was it. I could feel my heart thumping hard in my chest.

I tried to sneak into the back bedroom to take the call. Brian followed, taking out his phone to record the moment. The rest of my family scurried into the kitchen, pretending that they weren't listening in. I hit the screen to take the call.

"You're in," Amanda said immediately. "You got the invite. You're going to Rio."

I tried to take a deep breath, worried that I might hyperventilate.

"You're sure?"

"Yes, Melissa, I'm sure. You're going."

I wasn't sure at first exactly how to react. I had been on edge for weeks. I also realized that I had less than a month before I'd need to fly to Rio.

I questioned her a few more times and finally made the decision to believe her. I clicked off the phone, and I allowed myself a big smile. I walked out of the back bedroom into the kitchen to the sight of my entire family waiting with wide eyes. I threw my arms up in the air.

"I'm in!" I shouted. Everyone went absolutely nuts. My parents jumped up and down; Jake sprinted around in circles with his tail high. Brian looked like he was struggling to keep his feet on the ground as he kept filming everything with his phone.

When I look back from the end of my life, whenever that happens, I know that will be one of my best days. I had given birth to Dallas and then worked so hard to qualify for the Paralympics, and it worked. I've probably watched Brian's video a thousand times since then.

When the celebration died down, my sister came into the kitchen with a cake that had *Rio 2016* written in frosting—she'd made it ahead of time, and, if I didn't get the invite, the plan was to scrape off the top and we'd eat it anyway. I sat with Brian and Dallas, feeding my sweet tooth and starting to call everybody I knew.

Twenty minutes later, Amanda called back.

"Hey, don't tell anybody yet," she said. "They haven't made the official announcement yet. Hold off until after that."

I had pretty much already told the whole world.

Oops.

Chapter 28

On Top of the World

At the end of August, I traveled with the U.S. Paratriathlon team to Pensacola, Florida, where we spent four days at a pre-games camp before flying to Rio. When we finally got to Brazil, we were greeted with an extremely warm welcome, but the organizers hadn't combed through and figured out every detail like those in Beijing in 2008. There were still signs up for the Olympics rather than the Paralympics, and the athletes' village wasn't quite up to par. We felt there was a struggle for Paralympic athletes to be positioned on the same level as our fully able counterparts.

I shared a suite with my teammates on the eighth floor of the Team USA building, and six of us ended up all having to share one bathroom where toilet paper wouldn't flush. It was an uneasy start to what was going to be the biggest competition of my life. We felt lucky, though—the Paratriathlon venue was a two-hour drive away, and we knew we'd only have to stay there the first four nights before we were relocated to a closer hotel.

I knew and felt much closer to my paratriathlon teammates than my swimming teammates, and I couldn't wait to walk with them in the Opening Ceremony. Hailey and I hung out at the back of our Team USA delegation as we met the athletes from other countries, trading pins and soaking up the feeling of celebration.

For the second time in my life, I walked through the tunnel into the packed stadium, accompanied by the roar of cheers and the chants of *USA! USA!* Hailey and I started dancing, moving around the stadium to our own rhythm, feeling the power of so many people from so many countries gathered in competition. We moved to the beat of Brazilian music, waving to the crowd, spotting our families—just an electric feeling that we wanted to last and last. I didn't have a race the next day like I had in Beijing, so I was able to just laugh and relax and try to absorb the moment.

A couple of days later, we were on charter buses to a hotel on the picturesque shore of Copacabana Beach. Stepping into the Marriott was a huge relief. I opened my hotel room door to a huge "Good Luck" banner on the wall and my entire bed filled with pictures and cards wishing me well—the work of our team manager, who had asked everyone's loved ones to share memories and words of encouragement to make us feel welcome.

The feeling in that moment drove home how crucial it is to have support from family and friends in one's journey through life—no matter how single-minded you are in pursuing your dreams, recognizing the meaning of the rest of life feeds those goals. After giving birth and working myself back into

Paralympic shape, I was calling this part of my journey the *Mommy Road to Rio.*

* * *

Mentally, I felt a lot more pressure in Rio than I had in Beijing. I was all in on my single event, rather than swimming in a handful of races spread out over a two-week period. Triathlon has so many variables and so many things that can go wrong. Your goggles can come off while you're swimming. You can get kicked in the face in the water—that happened a lot. Your wetsuit zipper might get stuck during transition, or you could get a flat tire on your bike (I knew about that one). A biking or running prosthetic could break or malfunction. (Check.)

I was trying not to think about any of those things leading up to my race. Instead, I focused and concentrated on all the training I'd put in—the preparation that creates a process and a feeling that everything will work out. I was also trying not to relive the feelings I'd experienced after my failure to medal in Beijing. Two days before the race, I had a chance to have dinner with fifteen of my friends and family who had made the trip to Rio. This was a welcome difference from Beijing, where I had been swimming almost every day and isolated from my loved ones until all my events were over.

Of all days, my race was on September 11. I woke up that morning alone in my hotel room and dedicated the first few minutes of the day to the meaning of this anniversary.

I gave thanks out loud for my life. I then gave a silent thanks and a remembrance of those who had made the ultimate sacrifice on that day. Knowing that I was going to race the biggest triathlon of my life on that anniversary gave an even deeper meaning to a day that always included solemn remembrance. I was going to swim every stroke, pedal every mile, and run every step, in dedication to those who had lost their lives. And the event was going to be my way of thanking every fallen soldier for their service.

I was wearing red, white, and blue when I met Keri in the Marriott lobby at five in the morning. She was bubbling with excitement and wearing a *Team Melissa* T-shirt. We took the ten-minute walk together over to the triathlon venue as the sun began to rise over Copacabana Beach.

The regularity and adherence to schedule that I learned in the military never really goes away, and so I always want to be the first in line when the pre-race check-in process begins—and I was the first one there that morning. I went to the transition area to start setting up my equipment while Keri worked her way up into the spectator stands to save space for all the Team USA fans who would be arriving a little later in the morning. I spotted her up above as I set up my bike and jumped in the ocean for a warmup swim.

As I got out of the water, I felt a rush of nerves hit me. I kept thinking about process and practice. Helping to ease my mind was Brian, who was waiting with my parents to give me a hug.

The stands had started to fill with spectators. I saw the blue carpet rolled out at the finish line. I ran over to my family in the stands, smiling and waving. I saw my friend, Tiffany, who had been my roommate in my freshman year of college and was still one of my best friends. I saw my sister, Amanda, my friends, Lauren, Tara, Dan, Brandi, Dave—so many were there to cheer me on. The nerves were okay. In the bigger picture, I was so happy to be there—I thought about how, a month before, it wasn't a given that I'd even be competing. The fact that it was September 11 made it feel as though it was meant to be.

When the race was about to begin, the announcer read out the names of each competitor. Allysa, Hailey, and I got big cheers—there was a large Team USA contingent giving us love and support.

"Time to shine," I told myself through the nerves.

We all swam out to a pontoon where we gathered before the start and got hydrated before the swim in the salty water. When we were just minutes from the starting horn, I looked over to Hailey—somehow her goggles had come apart.

"Can you help?" she asked.

That's friendship—one of my biggest competitors asking for help with her equipment before the biggest race of our lives. I helped her get her goggles to work, and then all the racers entered the water.

The countdown began, with blaring dramatic music. I could feel my heart pounding as the starting horn sounded.

I'd always been among the best swimmers in the triathlons I raced, but, since Dallas, I hadn't been able to take the lead in the water in any of the races I'd entered. Now I knew that my swim was going to have to be at its best if I was going to have a good race.

I got out in front, maneuvering successfully around the first buoy as the water churned with swimmers. I got around the second, working hard, feeling my body respond the way it had in the past.

What's going on? How am I out in front? Why is no one catching me?

I finished the swim in the lead—the fastest for the first time in a few years. I couldn't have asked for a better start.

On the beach, I put my arms around one of the water exit handlers who helped us out of the water to our legs. I made my way to a chair where I took off my wetsuit and put on my running leg to run to my transition—I got going before anyone else was even out of the water. I looked up to the spectator stands, where Brian and Keri and my family and friends were going crazy.

Maybe I'm going to do this.

When I got to my bike, I glanced back and Allysa, Hailey, and a racer from Japan were all behind me—but not so far behind. The swim was my strength, but the bike remained my weakest of the three events. I hopped on and got started, and then Hailey passed me—this was her best event. As hard as I worked, after two laps, Hailey had pedaled out of my sight.

Each lap brought me around to the deafening cheers of the crowd. I looked up and saw my people, feeling their support giving me the motivation to push each pedal stroke harder than the last. The second time I rode close to the crowd, I pulled something out of my sports bra and pressed it against my lips.

People in the stands probably assumed that it was a cross or a photo of my kid that I was kissing for good luck, but it was my blue tube of Chapstick, one that I kept tucked away for big races—it was my thing, just like it had been in Iraq. I rubbed my lips with water-logged Chapstick and kept pushing harder. By the third lap, Allysa had passed me and Hailey was leading by a pretty significant margin. But, by the fourth and final lap, I caught back up to Allysa We were almost in sync when we reached the transition zone.

I had won the swim. Hailey won the bike. Now the run: Allysa's strength.

Allysa took off like a rocket. I didn't even try to catch her—if I did, I'd blow out my legs and end up struggling to even finish.

I was in third place, about two minutes in front of Liisa Lilja from Finland.

My run is always very much hit or miss. I'm not the most consistent competitor, and I either have a great day or I don't.

I could tell right away that this run was going to be a struggle. It definitely wasn't going to be the fastest run of my life. I just needed to stay in front of Liisa, and that was going to require digging really deep.

As I rounded the end of the first lap, my cheering section stood up and I saw the most amazing thing: They were bobbing jumbo-sized cutouts of Dallas's face as inspiration. It was almost as though he was there cheering me on.

My eyes darted across the course and caught a glimpse of Allysa passing Hailey. I was about thirty seconds behind them and Liisa was now about a minute behind me—and, while Hailey and Allysa were getting farther away from me, Liisa was gaining ground. My only goal at that point was not to let Liisa catch up to me. Hailey and Allysa had pretty much locked down the top two spots, and, if I could just hold on, then we would be able to pull off an all-USA-sweep of the event.

The thought of an all-American podium propelled me through the first half of the last lap. I looked over and saw a profusely sweating Brian pacing up and down the sideline—he looked even more frantic than me. I felt so profoundly that we were a team, and, when there was about half a mile left in the run, I heard him shouting.

"You're only three minutes out of first place!" he yelled. "You can do this!"

Really, Brian?

I knew, by that point, that I wasn't going to win the race. I just wanted to complete the USA sweep. I was trying to hold back laughter, loving his unwavering belief in me, as I kept pushing my pace.

"I don't care where first is!" I called to him. "Where's fourth?"

At the final turn of the course, I saw the blue carpet rolled out that marked the finish. When I reached it, it meant there were just 200 meters to go.

From the side of the course, I saw Tiffany, who shouted, "Finland is right behind you!"

I had pictured hitting the blue carpet and taking in the atmosphere of the people in the stands and the sun reflecting off the blue water beyond the track. But now I had to light a fire inside myself. I hit a sprint, running as fast as I possibly could while I pushed to the finish. Allysa and Hailey were waiting there with an American flag.

It's going to happen. It's really going to happen. We're going to do this.

I crossed the finish line and fell into Hailey and Allysa's arms as they wrapped the American flag around the three of us. We hugged and screamed and jumped up and down and chanted, *U-S-A! U-S-A!* I was out of control with excitement.

There were cameras everywhere. I stopped to talk to NBC.

"This is a great result for paratriathlon in the United States," I told the reporter. "But we also were able to show what the United States is capable of achieving on the anniversary of September 11."

I was the happiest bronze medalist in Rio. I didn't care that I wasn't taking home the gold or silver. I had wanted to earn a spot on the medalist's podium, and that's what I did. Our historic sweep was larger than just me.

Ecstatic with energy, I went off to find my family. I had thought my energy was spent after sprinting to the finish line, but I got a second wind, and then I got a third. I was running around all the people gathered close to the finish, and the poor doping official had to follow me to keep up—her job was to keep me in sight from the moment I finished the race until I was done with drug testing. I ran around the spectator bleachers, and that's where I saw Brian sprinting toward me—I ran to him and leapt into his arms.

I was shrieking at the top of my lungs, shaking with happiness, and I could tell that Brian was trying to figure out if I was upset with my race. I was crying and holding him and crying even harder when my family found us and we all embraced. The tears wouldn't stop.

In Beijing, I had cried because of how unhappy I was with my performance. On this day, I was crying from sheer happiness, totally overwhelmed by the intensity of what I felt. The bronze was my personal gold. I was there with the people I loved, and I had made it back.

Aside from having my kids, this was the greatest moment of my life.

Allysa, Hailey, and I were hugging and laughing through tears as we put on our Team USA gear for the podium ceremony. We stood together in the ready room, looking into each other's eyes.

"We did it, we did it," we kept repeating to each other.

Our hearts were swelling. The moment meant so much. We had shown our country, and the world, how much ability there is in a disability.

* * *

I was the first of the three to make my way up to the medal ceremony. My family and friends erupted as I stepped up to the podium and accepted my Paralympic bronze medal. Hailey and Allysa joined to accept silver and gold. The three of us huddled together with our medals around our necks as the national anthem began to play, and three American flags were raised above our heads.

I cried even more tears of joy.

It wasn't just me up there on that podium.

It was Brian. It was Dallas. It was my parents, my family, my good friends. It was my coaches and teammates. It was sponsors and supporters. It was my fellow soldiers. It was the doctors and nurses who had given me a second chance at life.

Twelve years before, I had almost lost my life in Iraq. I just lost my leg. That didn't take away my spirit. With love and support, and with will and belief, I had come back from the darkest moments of pain and doubt. I hoped others would see that they could fight back against whatever challenges life placed in front of them and that they would find their own power the way life had brought me to mine.

Allysa and Hailey and I gathered together at the top of the podium to pose for pictures. We were all thinking about the journeys the others had gone through. We all knew how long the road had been.

We danced and celebrated until they finally had to kick us out.

* * *

I had been away from Dallas for two weeks, and I couldn't wait to get home and show him the medal that I had barely taken off since that ceremony. On the flight home to Chicago, the pilot upgraded us to First Class after he spotted it. I couldn't figure out the best place to put the medal during the flight, so I just held it.

"Let me hold that," Brian said after a while, leaning over. "You need to sleep."

I finally was able to get some rest after the electricity of Rio, but I'd still wake up every hour and ask him where my medal was. *It's all really happening. I'm not dreaming.*

Back home, I walked into our duplex where Brian's mom was watching Dallas. He was two at the time and didn't entirely understand where I had been or what I had been doing.

"Look, Dallas," I said, holding up the medal for him to see. "I won this. I won this for you."

He took the medal and shook it happily. I put it around his neck and that was that. That was the culmination of the Mommy Road to Rio. Mothers are even tougher than you think.

* * *

Later that night, I rewarded myself by sitting on our living room floor eating an enormous chocolate chip skillet cookie all by myself in a single sitting. My sweet tooth was totally satisfied.

I spent the weekend at home, and, when Monday arrived, Brian went back to work and our nanny arrived to take care of Dallas. I suddenly didn't know what to do, since I had been used to training every single day for the Paralympics, so I put my bronze medal in my pocket and wandered aimlessly around our neighborhood streets. I stopped to buy scones and coffee three or four different times that day, just reflecting on everything that had happened and letting memories flow through me.

A week later, I let Dallas play with my medal again, and he ended up throwing it against my prosthetic leg. My leg was harder, and it dented the bronze medal. I was upset for about twenty seconds.

Oh well, it just gives it character.

I'll forever have a Paralympic bronze with a little dent in it, courtesy of my son. That medal represents all of the best choices I ever made.

And the dent really does give it character.

Chapter 29

Never Say Never

I had the thought every day: *What do I do now?*

After Rio, I felt a lot like I had after Beijing. The daily training routine was gone. While it was a relief, it left me with a lot of unstructured downtime—and I had pretty strong opinions about downtime.

Brian and I had known for a while that we wanted to have another child. There was a thing already starting to happen that we jokingly called the post-Rio Baby Boom: A lot of athletes, not to mention coaches and others involved with the Rio Paralympics, had put off having children until the total devotion of preparing for the games was in the past.

We ended up being part of the Boom. I was pregnant before the end of the year, pretty much right away—and, this time, unlike with Dallas, I knew what to expect and had been looking for the signs. This time out, we decided we wouldn't find out the gender until the birth.

I had given that first graduation speech all the way back in 2006, and now I was making a good part of my living as a public speaker—telling my story from Baghdad to Beijing and beyond. This part of my work got even more serious after winning my bronze in Rio. I started working with a marketing agency called Chicago Sports and Entertainment and got busier traveling to speak to business groups and others who wanted to hear about my experiences and the choices I had made to overcome adversity.

To be honest, I was enjoying not having to be as strict about working out as I had when I was training for the Paralympics. I was able to more present as a mother with Dallas, who was growing up fast. In between the public speaking, I got back into coaching—Dare2Tri was growing even faster than I could have imagined. We were able to take our programming to the next level with year-round training and three camps throughout the year that were servicing more than 300 athletes. We were making a real name in the triathlon scene, and I loved the feeling of growing into a mentor for the generation coming up behind me.

I tried to stay in shape, and did a decent job, but, between my work, being a mom, being pregnant again, and being a wife, I managed to stay busy without a single-minded focus on training.

Our daughter, Millie, was born on August 2, 2017. Her name is Amelia Lynn, but she's always been Millie to us. She, too, was born via C-section, but, this time, I knew it in advance. We had everything scheduled and planned out.

I learned, though, that Millie does things on her terms. I went into labor early, and she was in a breech position—there were moments when it felt like an emergency, but the doctors and nurses kept us safe.

She took my breath away from the moment I saw her. She is beautiful, with gorgeous dimples. And she was feisty from her first scream—and continues to be. A lot of daughters are like that—me included, according to my parents—and I could see a strength in her that I hope will serve her well for her entire life. With Dallas and Millie, our family was complete.

* * *

My new coach was named Chris Palmquist, and she had me training during the pregnancy, I was running until seven months in, and I was swimming up until the day before I had Millie. The Tokyo Paralympics were coming up in 2020. I wasn't sure if I wanted to try to get there, but I would at least stay in decent shape, so it wouldn't be as difficult to get there if I decided that was what I wanted.

The five of us—me, Brian, Dallas, Jake, and now Millie—moved to a suburb called Western Springs. We bought a house on a tree-lined street with amazing neighbors. I was a suburban mom with two kids, trying to figure life out like everybody else.

Then, one day, I woke up and decided that I wanted to give 2020 and the Tokyo Paralympics a shot.

It was a decision that I had to make with Brian. There would be a lot of sacrifice for all of us, and a lot of time devoted to try and make that a reality.

"I still love the sport," I told my husband. "I love the fitness, the thrill, and the camaraderie. I think I can still do it, so why not give it another chance?"

It helped that our kids were still young enough that they didn't have a lot of activities of their own going on outside the house—no school yet, no organized sports. I wouldn't be missing out on all those important memories if I gave this a shot.

Getting back in shape was just as hard as it had been after I had Dallas. Chris was an amazing coach at helping me try to maintain a balance between family and training. And, like before, I had to start with the goal of running just one mile.

I put the kids to bed, put on my headlamp, and went out there myself. The first night, I could only run a few minutes. But I went out again and again and finally ran that one mile. I did it again the next night.

Like the last time, I was easier on myself than I would have been when I was younger. One bad workout didn't mean I had destroyed my hopes of making the team. Once Millie was old enough for daycare, I fell into a welcome routine: wake up, take the kids to daycare, train. Brian was still working as a prosthetist. I'd hit the road to travel for my speaking engagements.

In 2018, I started racing again on the international paratriathlon circuit. I was improving. But I wasn't improving as much as I wanted. I wanted to wake up one morning and be in the same shape as I'd been at Rio, but it wasn't happening. While I was having Millie, my competitors had gotten even faster, and I had even more catching up to do. I was frustrated, but still trying to take things a little at a time—trying to be happy with whatever progress I was making.

Right before Halloween, I got an email. There was a resident paratriathlon training program at the Olympic Training Center. Hopefuls for Tokyo could live and train there, full time—just like in 2008. I looked at that email for a few minutes, then got apprehensive. I archived it in my files.

No way can I move my family.

I knew how great the atmosphere would be, and how much progress I would make in my training, but it wasn't just me anymore. I couldn't just pick up and go the way I had a decade before.

In early November, we flew to Colorado, so Brian could deliver Jack a new prosthetic leg; Hailey, who was already living at the Olympic Training Center, got in touch and invited me to join the team training at the Center for a swim workout. I said, "Sure."

That was one of the most intense workouts ever for me. The altitude, being in the training environment with my main competitors—none of it was easy. *This is why they're getting faster and I'm not. Maybe this is where I need to be.*

Finally, I told Brian about the email. "It's too much right?" I said. It's a lot for our family. We shouldn't do it, right?"

Brian looked me in the eyes. "Let's do it," he said.

I did a double-take.

This husband of mine: my dreams became his dreams.

"If you don't do it, you'll always wonder, 'What if?'" he told me. So, the following week, I applied, pausing briefly before hitting the send button, and got accepted the following week. The next month was a blur. We flew back out to Colorado Springs to find a rental house, packed up our house in Illinois, placed a for rent sign in the front yard, and, a couple of days into the New Year, a moving truck was parked in our driveway. I'll never forget Dallas looking out the front door at the huge truck and tearfully asking, "They're going to bring all my toys, right?"

In Colorado Springs, our rental house ended up being only a mile from Jack's family, and they helped ease us into the transition. I had a feeling of things coming full circle.

* * *

I started the residency program on January 7. I'll never forget the date. I dropped the kids off at daycare and went to the Olympic Training Center. I found myself feeling incredibly emotional—so much change was happening, including Jake having passed away before we moved and still missing him. I was nervous but excited. The road kept unfolding in front of me, with so many new chapters.

The training program under my new coach Derick Williamson was intense. I was there with six others, including Hailey and Allysa, my main competitors, and the three of us pushed each other every day. We were friends while we were training, with the understanding that we also wanted to beat each other when race day came.

In 2019, I raced on the international circuit, and my times started to get better. The training, the daily hard work, and the altitude were paying off. My world rankings started to go up gradually until, by the end of the year, I was ranked fifth in the world.

There were now three of us in the top five, which was amazing. Just like before Rio, it was Allysa, Hailey, and then me. But, just like before, only two of us would get to qualify for Tokyo and the third was going to have to hope for an invite. There was no way of predicting what might happen in early 2020, but my suspicion was that I would need to hope for another invited slot. I kept training with my heart set on making the team.

At the end of 2019, our "temporary" move to Colorado became permanent and we bought a house. The mountains drew us in. The air, the way we could almost walk out our back door and hike with the kids—it was home for us now. We bought a house, and Brian and I decided to start a business.

We opened a prosthetics company called Tolsma/Stockwell Prosthetics in Colorado Springs, fitting amputees with artificial limbs and hoping to specialize in high-end prosthetics, fitting elite-level athletes.

It was scary but exciting. We had such an amazing network of friends back in Chicago, and that was almost enough to keep us from moving—it's rare, for instance, to ever find and live so close to a friend like Keri. But we knew we'd build something new in Colorado.

Dallas quickly made new friends and is starting kindergarten in the fall of 2020. As for Millie, her smile continues to woo anyone who crosses her path, and she sure keeps us on our toes. As my mom said, "She knows what she wants, and she wants it yesterday."

Like me. It'll serve her well.

I couldn't be part of Dare2Tri's daily operations anymore, but I still travel to Chicago for the big events, and my hope is that, after Tokyo, I'll be able to open a Dare2Tri chapter in Colorado.

I feel so fortunate every day. I wake up, I do things I love. I challenge myself as an athlete and as a parent.

After 2020, my Paralympic career will probably be over, but I'll still do triathlons as long as my body lets me. After that, *who knows?* I'll coach. I'll compete. I'll speak. I'll be a mom and a wife. There will always be another challenge. Maybe I'll swim the English Channel. Maybe I'll climb a mountain. I'll keep moving, keep feeling that wind and keep finding new ways to push myself.

Maybe I'll take up golf. Maybe it will be a Paralympic sport before too long. Never say never. I'll just be excited to see where it goes.

Epilogue

My Life Today

Every April 13, still, we gather together to celebrate my Alive Day and Little Leg's Birthday.

I've come to honor Little Leg's birthday even more than my actual birthday. It means more. It's a time to reflect on what it means to still be alive after the bomb. The invitation list expands every year—once you're on the list, you're always on the list.

I never feel sad or mad on Little Leg's birthday. There's no, *What if this? What if that?* I've done more with my life with one leg than I ever did with two.

And Alive Day is more than just a revelry for me, my life, and for Little Leg. It's a celebration of everybody's lives. We all get caught up in insignificant things, the little ways that life goes wrong. Alive Day is an annual reminder to pause, reflect, and appreciate what we have. Those of us who are still here have the power to make choices and to embrace the gift of being alive.

* * *

So many people from my story are still in my life. My closest friends and family. My teammates, my competitors.

There's Dawn Halfaker, Danielle Greene, and Tammy Duckworth, my fellow wounded soldiers from Ward 57 at Walter Reed. The four of us became a tight-knit support system, and we called ourselves the "Band of Mothers" when we were featured on *The Today Show* after we all had kids within a year of each other. We all went on to accomplish great things with our lives and we reunited with our kids at Little Leg's tenth birthday party.

There are my fellow soldiers from Iraq. We get to keep in touch, thanks to social media. We bonded over our shared experience and our shared patriotism, and I always love seeing updates on where their lives have gone, and their triumphs small and large.

There's Sergeant Pavich, a man who I never knew well at all until the day he saved my life after that roadside bomb. One day, I got a call from an unknown number, and, when I picked it up, I heard a voice say, *"Is that you, ma'am?"*

I knew who it was instantly. We talked and re-lived that day, and I thanked him as much as it's possible to thank someone who saved your life. We still talk a few times a year and hope to meet again in person someday.

There's Jack, who I met when he first lost his leg as a boy and came to a triathlon meeting with his dad. Today Jack is a sixteen-year-old superstar and a Dare2Tri Ambassador who competed at his first national championships in 2019 and took second place. His once skeptical mother, Heidi, is a great friend and the first to tell you that Jack can do absolutely anything. I still serve as one of his coaches and Brian makes his prosthetic legs. I have no doubt he's going to become a Paralympian one day.

I am no longer in contact with Dick, but, wherever he is, I hope he is happy. If I ever run into him, I'll walk over with a genuine hug and with no ill will over what happened between us. He was a large part of my story, and I will forever be grateful to him.

And Jake. Oh, Jake—a dog I still think about every day, leaving a hole in my heart that has yet to be filled. We think of getting another dog but I'm not sure it would ever live up to the dog Jake was. He is so dearly missed.

Lastly are those who are no longer with us, whose memory we honor and keep by continuing to push forward, to meet life's challenges, and to love and to live with open hearts.

I truly feel like the luckiest girl alive.

* * *

We all have that power—to make our lives what we want them to be, and to feel like the luckiest people alive. We have the power to choose to embrace change instead of resisting it. We have the power to find motivation in our adversity. We can adapt and thrive in life. We have the power to take charge of our destinies, however difficult it might seem, and to live our lives in ways that make the stories we want to share with and inspire the world.

I hope that my story helps you along your way.

AFTERWORD

On Tuesday, March 17, the U.S. Paratriathlon team gathered at 7:30 a.m. and swam in the state-of-the art swimming pool at the Olympic Training Center, as we'd done every morning for over a year. We talked about how lucky we were to still be able to swim while so many other pools around the nation had closed due to COVID-19. We felt a collective sense of pride as we got out of the pool that day. We also had a sense of calm knowing that, at the OTC, athletes always come first, and the staff would do everything they could to help us be the best athletes we could be. Fast-forward twelve hours to the news that the OTC—and all the facilities that we'd been using daily—would be off-limits for at least four weeks. We were shocked as we rushed to clear our lockers, but confident that we could adapt. We made training plans with our coach that involved biking and running outside, and setting up home gyms to include training exercises that improve swimming.

A week later, it was announced that the Olympic and Paralympic Games had been postponed until 2021. We all knew it was possible, but the thought of it actually happening seemed improbable. Not just because of what the games mean to the international sporting community, but because we'd all been training with a single goal in sight: Tokyo 2020. We were so close, the finish line within reach. While the International Olympic Committee's decision was the right decision—health should always come first—it made many athletes, including myself, reassess their life timelines, causing many of us to ask whether waiting another year is realistic. For most of us, an Olympic or Paralympic dream requires many sacrifices. Sometimes it's living paycheck to paycheck, or taking time away from family to train or race. Maybe it's putting off having a family until after the games, or hanging on day by day, hoping that your body holds up for one more go-round. One more year can feel like nothing to some athletes, but an eternity to others.

As you know, I moved my husband and two young kids out to Colorado in early 2019 to train at the Olympic Training Center in hopes of making it to Tokyo. Along the way I turned forty, opened a prosthetic business with my husband, and limited my speaking engagements so I could train and pursue my Tokyo dream. We were counting down the months until I could spend more time at our new office, spend more time with the kids and not be gone for weeks at a time, and pursue more speaking opportunities to bring in more income. (Not to mention a body that feels its age every morning!) But when I really thought about it, those thoughts were fleeting, ones that immediately popped to the surface but were quickly overtaken by the desire to see a dream through to its completion. One year—that's it! I quickly chose to take this opportunity and do the best I could with it, spend more time with my family, take on the home projects I've put off, and do my best to help my community, all while maintaining my training as best I can.

While this situation was far different from losing a leg, the disappointment we felt was still something similar. None of us ever imagined we would have these dreams postponed by a full year. None of us ever imagined we would be sitting in our homes for weeks on a stay-at-home order to flatten the curve and reduce the spread of the virus. But, it happened, and we all had the power of choice in how we dealt with it. That's the beauty of life. Having a choice in how we deal with unknown obstacles that cross our paths.

So, while this postponement was not in our plans, I've chosen to make the most of it—focus on my family's health and be thankful for it. For us athletes, it's knowing that even though the year has changed, the dream hasn't. When Tokyo *does* happen, it will be a celebration of sport and the endurance of the human spirit that will bring the world together. I have no doubt it will be worth the wait.

ACKNOWLEDGMENTS

Writing a book is a daunting task and it's certainly something I wouldn't have been able to do on my own. While it is my story there were so many people that helped me bring it to life.

First, I would like to thank Stuart Lieberman and Quinton Skinner for taking my spoken words and putting them down on paper. And thanks to everyone at Post Hill Press for reading my story and believing that others will also want to read it.

Secondly, I wouldn't have my story to tell if it weren't for those who believed in me and encouraged me to pursue my dreams. My parents are at the top of that list. And then Dick, my ex-husband, who believed I could not only persevere through the loss of my leg but stood by my side as I did it. And to all of those I served with who showed me firsthand what it means to be loyal to the country I live in and to be a true American.

To my fellow wounded veterans, my teammates, my coaches, and my sponsors who have believed in and taken a chance on me. To all my friends who were, and still are, part of my story. To Keri and Stephanie, whose daily talks keep me grounded and so full of life. My story is only here because of all of you.

Lastly, to my family.

My husband Brian who knew the importance of me spending hours on the phone every Tuesday night to get my story down on paper because he wanted me to share it with the world as much as I did. And for helping me write my story after I felt like I had lost it. For loving me and making me feel like the most beautiful girl in the world. I am so lucky my story includes you, my honeybee.

And sweet Dallas and Millie. You're still young enough to not yet understand the impact you have had on my life. Making it one filled with more love and more laughter and teaching me more about life than you may ever understand. I am so lucky to be your momma and I can't wait to help both of you write your stories and to encourage you to be whatever it is you want to be.

I am one lucky girl.

ABOUT THE AUTHOR

Born a patriot, Melissa Stockwell was the first female to lose a limb in active combat when a roadside bomb exploded under her vehicle while serving in Iraq. She considered herself one of the lucky ones, as she only lost her left leg and not her life. After receiving both a purple heart and a bronze star, she vowed to live her life for those who had given the ultimate sacrifice. After learning to walk again, Melissa went on to proudly become a two-time Paralympian, a three-time World Champion, and a Paralympic bronze medalist. She has received a number of accolades for her athletic success and has jaw-dropping moments, such as standing in a room with five presidents, sharing a dance with George W. Bush, and more. Melissa co-founded a nonprofit organization called Dare2tri which helps other athletes with physical disabilities get into the sport of triathlon. She also travels the world, sharing her story in hopes to inspire others and leave them with the notion that they have the power of choice regardless of what obstacles come their way. Her favorite job is being a mother to her two young kids, Dallas and Millie, and a wife to her husband, Brian. Melissa is a patriot in the truest sense and proves—time and time again—that we can all come out better on the other side of any challenge that comes our way.